Beacon of
HATRED

INSIDE HIZBALLAH'S
AL-MANAR TELEVISION

Avi Jorisch

WASHINGTON INSTITUTE FOR NEAR EAST POLICY

© 2004 by The Washington Institute for Near East Policy

Published in 2004 in the United States of America by The Washington Institute for Near East Policy,
1828 L Street NW, Suite 1050, Washington, DC 20036.

Library of Congress Cataloging-in-Publication Data

Jorisch, Avi, 1975–
  Beacon of hatred : inside Hizballah's Al-Manar Television / by Avi Jorisch.
    p. cm.
  ISBN 0-944029-88-4
1. Al-Manar (Television Network) 2. Hizballah (Lebanon) 3. Television and politics—Lebanon.
4. Arab-Israeli conflict—Mass media and the conflict. 5. Terrorism—Middle East. I. Title.

PN1992.92.A42J67 2004
384.55'455'095692—dc22
                          2004005382

THE AUTHOR
Avi Jorisch

Avi Jorisch was a Soref fellow at The Washington Institute for Near East Policy from 2001 to 2003, specializing in Arab and Islamic politics. More recently, he served as an Arab media and terrorism consultant for the Department of Defense.

Mr. Jorisch holds a bachelor's degree in history from Binghamton University and a master's degree in Islamic history from the Hebrew University of Jerusalem. In 2000–2001, he studied Arabic and Islamic culture through the Center for Arabic Studies Abroad program at the American University in Cairo. He also earned a certificate in Arabic after participating in an intensive summer program at al-Azhar University, the preeminent institution of Sunni Islamic learning.

Mr. Jorisch has traveled extensively in the Middle East, including Syria, Lebanon, Jordan, Israel, Gaza, the West Bank, Egypt, Qatar, Turkey, and Morocco. In addition, he has written at length about Hizballah, al-Manar, and related subjects, with articles appearing in prominent publications such as the *Los Angeles Times, Washington Times, Jerusalem Times,* and *Middle East Quarterly.*

TABLE OF CONTENTS

ACKNOWLEDGMENTS

This monograph is the culmination of two years of research that included watching countless hours of al-Manar programming, conducting numerous interviews in Lebanon and Qatar, and holding innumerable discussions with colleagues. I am grateful to The Washington Institute and the Helen and Samuel Soref Foundation for providing me with the resources and time to complete this study. In particular, I would like to thank Ambassador Dennis Ross, the Institute's executive director during my stay there, for maintaining an open-door policy and taking a real interest in my development. I would also like to thank Robert Satloff, then-director of policy and strategic planning, and Patrick Clawson, deputy director, for tirelessly supporting my research. In addition, I am indebted to Jonathan Schanzer, Amy Hawthorne, Steven Cook, Martin Kramer, Matthew Levitt, and my father, Henry Jorisch, for reading the manuscript—often more than once—and editing it at various stages.

I am also grateful to Jeffrey Starr for acting as my coach during the final stages of the project; to Jamil Mroue for our insightful conversations in Beirut and Washington; to Avi Lichter for all his help and for the gift of his friendship; to my late teacher Ehud Sprinzak, who planted one of the seeds for this study; to Mouafac Harb for going above and beyond; to Emma Freedman for teaching me the power of observation; to Daniel Nassif, Leah Odinec, Habib Malik, and Alan Makovsky for their encouragement and for providing me with some very helpful clues; and to Los Warith, Linda Israeli, Ofer Efrati, Nevenka Korica, Nabila al-Asyuti, and Zeinab Ibrahim for their time, energy, and support.

I would also like to thank those officials and personnel from Hizballah, al-Manar, and other regional media outlets who agreed to be interviewed (several of whom asked to remain anonymous). They include Bilal Zaarour (al-Manar's programming manager), Ibrahim Musawi (editor-in-chief of al-Manar's English news desk), Nayef Krayem (al-Manar's general manager and chairman of the board), and Sheikh Hassan Izz al-Din (member of Hizballah's Political Council and the party's director for media relations). (All titles represent the officials' positions at the time of their interviews.) Additional thanks go to Sheikh Haidar for arranging these and other meetings.

This study required an immense amount of work on the part of my research assistants Seth Wikas, Jeff Cary, Ben Fishman, Evan Langenhahn, and several others who have asked not to be named but whose contribution I greatly appreciate. I am also grateful to Alicia Gansz, George Lopez, and Alexis Luckey, the Institute's publications staff, for their professional skill and immense patience—I could not have asked for better editors. Finally, my sincere thanks go out to the many other friends, family members, and colleagues who labored in anonymity but whose contribution was invaluable to this work.

Avi Jorisch
Washington, D.C.
August 2004

FOREWORD

Internationally, Hizballah's terrorist activities and reputation are well known; indeed, Deputy Secretary of State Richard Armitage referred to the organization as "the A-team" of terrorism. Far less well known is the fact that Hizballah maintains a frighteningly slick satellite television channel, al-Manar, whose persistent messages of incitement and glorification of violence are watched throughout the Middle East.

In the first serious, analytical exposé of al-Manar, Avi Jorisch has provided a real service. He points out that much of the station's programming—whether in the form of news reports, music videos, talk shows, dramas, documentaries, or other genres—propagates specific themes that are in line with Hizballah's radical ideology. One such theme is the destruction of Israel through ongoing low-intensity violence and through demographic trends that favor the region's Arab population. Other themes highlight the glory of those fighting against both Israel and the United States. For example, the station's music videos—which are geared toward a young audience—are designed to make suicide missions seem appealing and heroic.

Clearly, al-Manar is more than a news outlet; it is an active arm of Hizballah. It exists to foster Hizballah's agenda for the region. It socializes hatred and the spirit of enduring conflict. It rejects the very concept of peace between Arabs and Israelis, and it does so with programming that targets all ages. Indeed, during his many conversations in Lebanon with those who run al-Manar, Avi found that they were not reticent to talk about these guiding principles. Accordingly, this study allows their words—and, to an even greater extent, the language of al-Manar's programs—to speak for themselves. It also uncovers many of the station's Western and Arab sources of advertising. The book concludes with detailed recommendations on what might be done to blunt al-Manar's effectiveness.

For anyone concerned with the threat posed by Hizballah and the best means of advancing the war on terror, *Beacon of Hatred* is a very important study.

Ambassador Dennis Ross
Former U.S. special Middle East
coordinator for the peace process

AUTHOR'S NOTE

Most of the al-Manar Television footage examined for this study was collected from the beginning of 2002 through summer 2004. From January to April 2002, Washington Institute personnel recorded al-Manar programming on a daily basis during Lebanese primetime viewing hours (defined herein as 8:30 p.m. to 12:30 a.m. local time). In total, hundreds of hours were collected, watched, and then analyzed carefully.

In summer 2002, the author conducted interviews at al-Manar headquarters in Lebanon, at the offices of other Lebanese television stations, and at al-Jazeera headquarters in Qatar. Unless otherwise indicated, all quotes attributed to al-Manar and Hizballah personnel were obtained from the individuals in question during interviews conducted at the Beirut station on June 27–28, 2002. The titles attributed to these personnel represent the positions they held at the time of the interviews.

Institute personnel continued to monitor al-Manar programming regularly after these visits. The formal methodology of recording, watching, and thoroughly analyzing al-Manar footage was resumed during the run-up to the U.S. invasion of Iraq and throughout the war itself and its aftermath.

Avi Jorisch

ABOUT THE CD-ROM

This book includes a CD-ROM containing video clips from Hizballah's al-Manar Television (see inside back cover). The clips were excerpted from a wide variety of al-Manar programming, including talk shows, music videos, news broadcasts, documentaries, commercials, and other between-program filler material.

Each of the fifty-seven clips is referenced and discussed in the chapters that follow; their order of appearance on the CD-ROM matches their order of appearance in the text. All textual references to the CD-ROM are indicated with a ◉ symbol near the relevant passage, in addition to a highlighted parenthetical note.

Please note that the video and audio quality of the clips will vary widely regardless of the platform on which they are viewed. Most of this variance is attributable to the different media from which the clips were recorded prior to their transfer into digital CD-ROM format.

SYSTEM REQUIREMENTS

The files on this CD-ROM are compatible with Adobe Acrobat Reader versions 6.0.1 and higher.

Windows

- Intel® Pentium® processor
- Microsoft® Windows 98 Second Edition, Windows Millennium Edition, Windows NT® 4.0 with Service Pack 6, Windows 2000 with Service Pack 2, Windows XP Professional or Home Edition, Windows XP Tablet PC Edition
- 32MB of RAM (64MB recommended)
- 60MB of available hard-disk space
- Internet Explorer 5.01, 5.5, 6.0, or 6.1

Macintosh

- PowerPC® G3 processor
- Mac OS X v.10.2.2-10.3

- 32MB of RAM with virtual memory on (64MB recommended)
- 70MB of available hard-disk space

USING THE CD-ROM

Windows

Insert the CD-ROM into your compact disc drive. The disc will AutoRun and prompt you to install Adobe Acrobat Reader 6.0.1, if required. IMPORTANT: *During the installation process, if the Acrobat Reader Setup Wizard prompts you to either "Repair" or "Remove" the Acrobat Reader 6.0.1 program, click "Repair" and proceed with installation.* When installation is complete, AutoRun will open the CD-ROM welcome screen. Follow directions on screen as prompted.

Macintosh

OS 8.6–9.2:

IMPORTANT: Acrobat Reader 6.0.1 is not compatible with Macintosh OS 8.6–9.2 operating systems. Users will not be able to view the CD-ROM's welcome screen or menus. Insert the CD-ROM into your compact disc drive. Open the "Videos" folder and double-click on the individual .mpg files to play in Quicktime. *The numbered .mpg files correspond to the video clip numbers referenced throughout the book text.*

OS X:

Insert the CD-ROM into your compact disc drive. If you do not already have Acrobat Reader version 6.0.1 or higher, double-click on the ***AdbeRdr60_enu_full.dmg*** icon. After Acrobat Reader is installed, double-click on the *start.pdf* file to begin.

EXECUTIVE SUMMARY

Given the increasing popularity of satellite dishes in the Arab world, many analysts have suggested that television has become a force for Westernization in the region. Yet this technology can be used to propagate hate and conflict as readily as tolerance and understanding.

Al-Manar, Arabic for "the beacon," is the official television mouthpiece of the Lebanese Party of God, or Hizballah. The terrorist organization uses al-Manar—which it calls the "station of resistance"—as an integral part of its plan to reach not only the citizens of Lebanon, but also the broader Arab and Muslim worlds. Indeed, Hizballah is the first organization of its kind to establish its own television station and use it as an operational weapon.

STATION BACKGROUND

In 1991, shortly after Hizballah actively entered the Lebanese political scene, al-Manar was launched as a small terrestrial station. Although legally registered as the Lebanese Media Group Company in 1997, al-Manar has belonged to Hizballah culturally and politically from its inception. Today, the terrestrial station can reach Lebanon in its entirety and broadcasts programming eighteen hours daily. Moreover, al-Manar's satellite station, launched on May 25, 2000, now transmits twenty-four hours a day, reaching the entire Arab world and the rest of the globe through seven major satellite providers.

Al-Manar's popularity in the region is clearly high. Lebanese television officials assert that the station is the third most popular in the country, rising to number one when events heat up in southern Lebanon or the Palestinian territories. Similarly, Israeli sources report that al-Manar ranks second only to al-Jazeera in the West Bank and Gaza Strip.

Regarding financial support, Lebanese law prohibits local television stations from receiving funding from any source outside Lebanon (whether individuals or governments). Although al-Manar vociferously denies receiving any such funding, it is an open secret that Iran bankrolls the station. Al-Manar's annual budget currently stands at $15 million—nearly half the size of al-Jazeera's budget. The station also receives advertising revenue from both Arab and Western companies.

TARGETING THE UNITED STATES AND ISRAEL

Following Israel's May 2000 withdrawal from its self-declared security zone in southern Lebanon, both Hizballah and al-Manar shifted their focus from the Lebanese arena to the Israeli-Palestinian arena. This transformation became especially noticeable after the outbreak of the Palestinian intifada in September 2000.

Today, Hizballah continues to use al-Manar as a means of publicly offering its services to Palestinians fighting for the destruction of Israel and the total liberation of historic Palestine (i.e., all territory west of the Jordan River). With one of its avowed activities being "psychological warfare against the Zionist enemy," Hizballah has effectively linked its own fate with that of the Palestinians, relying on the fight against Israel for much of its regional legitimacy and influence. Accordingly, one of al-Manar's major objectives is to inspire resistance. Since the start of the intifada, the station has also served as the first medium through which many Palestinian terrorist groups claim responsibility for suicide attacks against Israelis.

With regard to the United States, al-Manar has broadcast anti-American propaganda since its inception, often using the same propaganda methods it employs against Israel. Various programs have focused on distorting U.S. history, lambasting U.S. Middle East policy, propagating conspiracy theories about the September 11 attacks, and demonizing the relationship between Washington and the "Zionist entity," Israel. With the start of Operation Iraqi Freedom in 2003, both Hizballah and al-Manar renewed their vitriol toward their old, reliable foe, the "Great Satan." Throughout the war and its aftermath, the station's news programs, talk shows, and propaganda videos focused on U.S. aggression in the region and openly called for suicide attacks and other acts of resistance against U.S. targets.

PROGRAMMING CONTENT

Al-Manar programming skillfully combines news, talk shows, documentary series, propaganda music videos, and other elements. Much of this programming boasts a professional appearance, impressive-looking sets, handsomely dressed anchors, and well-written and well-delivered scripts.

News. Al-Manar broadcasts eight Arabic news bulletins daily, in addition to one English and one French bulletin. Besides its headquarters in Beirut, the station has news bureaus in Egypt, Iran, Jordan, and the United Arab Emirates (Dubai). It also has correspondents in Belgium, France, Iraq, Kosovo, Kuwait, Morocco, the Palestinian territories, Russia, Sweden, Syria, Turkey, and the United States. In the eyes of the Arab world, this global presence lends the station substantial credibility. Al-Manar's unique ability to deliver news from the Palestinian territories—particularly following terrorist attacks—also serves to bolster its standing among viewers.

Primetime programming. Al-Manar's primetime lineup includes a number of self-produced talk shows, dramas, and documentaries, including the following:

- *The Spider's House* is a talk show dedicated in part to uncovering the weaknesses of the "Zionist entity." The program claims that Israel can be destroyed through a combination of low-intensity warfare and a demographic shift in favor of Arabs, the latter facilitated by implementing the Palestinian right of return to all of pre-1948 Palestine. In addition, since the U.S. invasion of Iraq, episodes have explored how to use violent resistance—including suicide bombing—to end the U.S. occupation.

- *What's Next* is one of several al-Manar political talk shows that feature guests espousing vitriolic anti-American views. Some of these guests are spokespersons for groups that the U.S. government has labeled Specially Designated Global Terrorist (SDGT) entities and Foreign Terrorist Organizations (FTOs).

- *My Blood and the Rifle* is a documentary series dedicated to glorifying Hizballah's guerrilla fighters and inspiring viewers to join the resistance against Israel.

- *Returnees* is a program dedicated to the Palestinian refugee problem. In keeping with Hizballah ideology, these individuals are referred to not as "refugees," but rather as "returnees" who are slated to reassume ownership of the lands that currently make up the state of Israel.

- *Terrorists* is a weekly documentary series highlighting perceived "terrorist acts" that Israel has perpetrated against the Arab world throughout history.

- *In Spite of the Wounds* is a documentary series dedicated to individuals who have been injured while fighting against Israel. Their sacrifices are glorified, as is their newfound status as pillars of society.

Music videos. Music videos *(anashid)* make up approximately 25 percent of al-Manar's programming. One of their primary purposes is to keep Arab anger focused on the Palestinian problem and the U.S. presence in Iraq. They also serve as reminders of Hizballah's willingness to lead the fight against Israel.

Al-Manar officials assert that they strive to create music videos with the level of professionalism that they see on U.S. television networks, specifically MTV. The videos themselves tend to feature violent images and incendiary language. By the station's own admission, these elements are meant to foster suicide operations by inciting individual viewers toward violence. For example, Ayat al-Akhras, a young Palestinian woman, reportedly watched al-Manar incessantly before blowing herself up in front of a Jerusalem supermarket in March 2002, killing two Israelis and wounding twenty-eight others.

Filler material. Al-Manar often broadcasts short sections of filler material in between full-length programs or during commercial breaks. This material serves several key functions, including the following:

- displaying addresses and bank account numbers to which viewers can send money in support of Hizballah;
- listing locations worldwide where demonstrations will soon take place;
- disseminating various inflammatory slogans in Arabic, English, or Hebrew (e.g., "In your death, you are victorious"; "Jerusalem is ours"; "The road to victory is resistance").

POLICY RECOMMENDATIONS

U.S. officials have made clear that Hizballah ranks high on the list of possible targets in the war on terror. In September 2002, for example, Deputy Secretary of State Richard Armitage called Hizballah the "A-team" of terrorism, suggesting that it constituted a greater threat to the United States than perhaps even al-Qaeda. Washington must now devote equal consideration to the mass media tools that Hizballah uses to further its agenda. The U.S. government should not underestimate the damaging effects of a television station that encourages violent activity such as suicide bombing in the guise of slick programming that appeals to all ages.

No measure—short of direct military confrontation—can silence al-Manar completely, particularly as long as Syria maintains its occupation of Lebanon and Iran continues its support of Hizballah's radical activities. Nevertheless, the U.S. government can take several steps to limit the scope and effectiveness of the station's propaganda efforts and make its operations far more difficult and costly:

- The Treasury Department should add al-Manar to its terrorism sanctions list.
- The United States should ask the four Lebanese banks that currently hold Hizballah bank accounts—and any other banks with which Hizballah does business— to freeze the accounts in question. If these banks refuse to comply, the Treasury Department's Office of Foreign Assets Control should designate them as institutions harboring accounts of a terrorist organization. This designation would allow Washington to freeze their U.S.-based assets and block their access to U.S. markets.

- The United States should take action against any American financial institutions that continue to serve as agents for noncompliant Lebanese banks.
- The Foreign Terrorist Asset Tracking Center—the intergovernmental task force responsible for uncovering terrorist financing—should begin monitoring al-Manar broadcasts for advertised bank accounts.
- The United States should enforce existing laws or pass new legislation prohibiting U.S. companies from advertising on any of Hizballah's mass media outlets.
- Washington should begin a dialogue with European Union officials regarding European companies that advertise on al-Manar.
- The United States should enforce existing laws or pass new legislation prohibiting U.S. media from purchasing footage from, or providing footage to, al-Manar. Washington should encourage Europe to do the same.
- The United States should enforce existing laws that ban U.S. citizens and companies from working with SDGT entities and FTOs. In doing so, the U.S. government should close down al-Manar's Washington bureau (housed within the Associated Press's Washington bureau) and consider pressing criminal charges against the bureau's chief, Muhammad Dalbah.
- The United States should investigate foreign firms that have provided assistance, including media training, to Hizballah or al-Manar.
- The United States should encourage foreign satellite package providers to remove al-Manar from their networks. It should also force IntelSat, a U.S.-based provider, to cease offering al-Manar.
- The United States should consider providing the Lebanese government with the intelligence and support it needs to enforce its own ban on foreign financing of Lebanese media.
- Washington should ask Iraqi authorities to remove al-Manar's correspondents from Iraq.
- In light of Syria's ongoing occupation of Lebanon, the United States should demand that Damascus end al-Manar's calls for suicide attacks on U.S. forces in Iraq and elsewhere. Syria's response should be treated as a central test for whether Damascus is cooperating in the war on terrorism.
- The United States should pressure Egypt, Iran, Jordan, and the United Arab Emirates to close down al-Manar bureaus. It should also pressure Belgium, France, Egypt, Iran, Jordan, Kosovo, Kuwait, Morocco, the Palestinian Authority, Russia, Sweden, Syria, Turkey, and the United Arab Emirates to forbid al-Manar correspondents from reporting on their soil.

Al-Manar's programming puts American lives at risk, both in Iraq and elsewhere, and hinders the prospects for peace and stability throughout the region. Washington must therefore expand its efforts to alter or silence the station's message. Only then will the United States be able to make serious headway in the battle of ideas in the Middle East.

INTRODUCTION

During the 1970s, when Ayatollah Ruhollah Khomeini was living in exile from Iran, cassette tapes of his sermons were passed along from one Shiite household to another, inspiring a generation to bring down the reigning Shah Muhammad Reza Pahlavi through an Islamic revolution. This phenomenon occurred largely under Washington's radar screen because relatively few government personnel spoke Persian or Arabic, and fewer still tracked this grass-roots medium of communication. If more American analysts had examined Khomeini's ideas and the dissemination of his sermons, the U.S. government might have been better prepared for the Iranian revolution.

A similar phenomenon is currently taking place in Lebanon. When Hizballah founded al-Manar Television in 1991, it launched a new kind of televised revolution—one that is now broadcast into millions of homes in the Middle East and beyond. Today, anyone in the region who possesses a satellite dish can watch al-Manar (Arabic for "the beacon") twenty-four hours a day, seven days a week. This powerful medium is Hizballah's primary method of spreading its message to a diverse audience beyond its traditional Lebanese Shiite followers. A direct outgrowth of Hizballah's desire to expand its influence, al-Manar serves as another front upon which the party wages its fight against both Israel and the United States.

Although al-Manar resembles traditional commercial television stations that broadcast serial programs, news programs, sports programming, family programming, and talk shows, the station's goal is to disseminate propaganda that promotes Hizballah's radical message of terrorism and other forms of violence, including suicide bombing. Hizballah openly calls for the destabilization of the region in order to disrupt the U.S.-sponsored Arab-Israeli peace process and to actualize the party's strategic vision. Accordingly, al-Manar's main website (www.manartv.com), which claims to wage "psychological warfare" against what it labels the "Zionist entity," explicitly advocates driving Jews out of historic Palestine.

For more than fifty years, the international community has recognized that the Israeli-Palestinian conflict can be resolved only through a two-state solution. Yet Hizballah, through al-Manar, advocates a one-state Palestinian solution that involves annihilating the

Jewish state via a combination of violent and passive means. Hizballah considers all land west of the Jordan River to be occupied by the Jewish people. Therefore, the organization regards all acts of violence against Israelis as legitimate resistance rather than terrorism. This ideology, expressed on al-Manar, fosters a heightened sense of instability in the region and rejects realistic, negotiated solutions to the Arab-Israeli conflict.

Regarding the United States—which Hizballah has called its "true and original enemy"—al-Manar programming has long propagated explicit messages meant to incite anger against U.S. foreign policy. With the commencement of Operation Iraqi Freedom in 2003, al-Manar intensified its hostile anti-American stance, directing much of its message of hate toward the United States and calling for resistance attacks against U.S. forces. Indeed, by broadcasting vitriolic messages and gruesome footage, al-Manar has shown its clear intention of fomenting anger at U.S. military operations in the region and advocating violent resistance. Moreover, using an abundance of speeches, propaganda videos, and talk shows highlighting the "inherent evil" of America's leaders and foreign policy, the station has continued to stir viewers' frustrations by blaming many of the region's problems on the United States and Israel. This type of programming promotes and celebrates an environment in which terrorist attacks such as those that took place on September 11, 2001, are acceptable political acts. Messages of this sort can lead only to increased attacks against Americans and U.S. interests throughout the region.

This book presents the messages of al-Manar in the network's own words in an effort to foster better understanding of Hizballah and its militant ideology. Ideally, this study will spark a debate among policymakers and citizens alike regarding how best to confront and defeat the threat that Hizballah poses to U.S. interests. As Washington reaches out to the Arab world through public diplomacy efforts such as the Middle East Partnership Initiative, Radio Sawa, and al-Hurra television, it must remain keenly aware of the radical messages it will need to counter. Al-Manar's sophisticated use of television technology must be skillfully rebutted if the United States is to make progress in the fight for the hearts and minds of Middle Easterners.

PART 1

HISTORY AND BACKGROUND

CHAPTER 1

HISTORY OF HIZBALLAH

Many Westerners regard the Lebanese group Hizballah as one of the most notorious terrorist organizations in the world. It has been held responsible for the 1983 terrorist attacks against the U.S. embassy and Marine barracks in Beirut; the 1992 and 1994 attacks against the Israeli embassy and Jewish cultural center in Buenos Aires; and a host of kidnappings, hijackings, and suicide bombings.

As a result of those and other activities, the U.S. State Department branded Hizballah a Foreign Terrorist Organization (FTO) in 1997.[1] Moreover, in the aftermath of the al-Qaeda attacks of September 11, 2001, Hizballah was labeled a Specially Designated Global Terrorist (SDGT) entity under Executive Order 13224.[2] This designation empowered the U.S. government to impose financial sanctions against those entities "that support or otherwise associate" with Hizballah. In addition, Executive Order 12947 and the International Emergency Economic Powers Act prohibited the provision of "financial, material, or technological support" to any specially designated terrorist group.[3]

More recently, Hizballah began to rhetorically threaten the U.S. presence in Iraq. During the buildup to the 2003 U.S. invasion of that country, Hizballah's leaders asserted that they were not interested in opening a second front. Sheikh Hassan Nasrallah, Hizballah's secretary-general, insisted, "Outside this fight [i.e., the Israeli-Palestinian arena], we have done nothing. Everybody knows where Hezbollah's arena is, where Hezbollah's battle is."[4] At the same time, however, Hizballah encouraged Arabs in general, and Iraqis specifically, to rise up and violently oppose the U.S. invasion and occupation.

Well before Operation Iraqi Freedom, Deputy Secretary of State Richard Armitage categorized Hizballah as a greater threat to the United States than even al-Qaeda, labeling it

5

the "A-team" of terrorism. Moreover, Senator Bob Graham, former chair of the Senate Intelligence Committee, has repeatedly asserted that the United States should have targeted Hizballah before going to war with Iraq. Now that Saddam Hussein's regime has been toppled, Washington has begun to consider its next potential target in the war on terror. Many analysts have concluded that Hizballah should be at the top of the list.

THE FOUNDING OF HIZBALLAH

Hizballah emerged as a result of four factors: the Lebanese civil war, the marginalization of the Lebanese Shiite community, the Islamic revolution in Iran, and the 1982 Israeli invasion of Lebanon. Well before Lebanon achieved full independence from the French in 1943, it had already undergone significant religious conflict. In an attempt to end strife among the country's eighteen religious denominations, the Lebanese government adopted a system that apportioned political power based on each religious group's demographic standing in the 1932 census.[5] Christian Maronites and Sunni Muslims were demographically dominant and were therefore accorded the two most influential positions: president and prime minister, respectively. The Shiites were granted the position of speaker of the parliament.

This arrangement worked relatively well until the 1970s, when considerable demographic shifts took place. Higher birthrates among Lebanese Sunnis encouraged many of them to call for greater representation. The Christians, however, perceived any political change as a threat to their power base and refused to allow a new census to take place. In 1975, the situation deteriorated into civil war. The country fragmented along religious lines, most dramatically in the capital, which was divided into Muslim and Christian sectors. In May 1976, Lebanon's Christian president, Elias Sarkis, asked President Hafiz al-Asad of Syria to send troops to Lebanon. That move began what is still widely perceived to be a Syrian occupation. (The Taif Accord, part of which called on Syria to end its occupation, was signed in 1989, but its provisions regarding Syrian withdrawal have yet to be implemented.)

Meanwhile, the growing Palestinian community in Lebanon exacerbated the country's civil strife. After being expelled from Jordan in 1970 following the events of Black September, Yasser Arafat and members of the Palestine Liberation Organization (PLO) settled in Beirut and Shiite-majority southern Lebanon, establishing a de facto state-within-a-state in the area. Soon thereafter, local Palestinians (most of whom were Sunni) began fighting with Shiites over scarce resources.

The PLO also waged guerrilla raids across Lebanon's southern border into Israel. These raids provoked harsh Israeli retaliation, compounding the already deteriorating situation in

Lebanon. In an attempt to stop the raids, Israel invaded Lebanon, first in 1978 and again in 1982. After forcing the PLO into exile in Tunis in 1982, Israel retained control of its self-proclaimed "security belt," a 410-square-mile swath of Lebanese territory, until its final withdrawal from the country in May 2000.[6]

Throughout this period, Lebanese Shiites were relatively deprived in comparison to members of other denominations, receiving scant government attention and inadequate access to social services. They looked for salvation in the form of Musa Sadr, an Iranian-born Shiite cleric of Lebanese descent. Sadr founded Amal, a secular reformist movement that quickly improved social, economic, and political conditions for the Lebanese Shiite community.[7] On a trip to Libya in 1978, however, Sadr disappeared, and many speculated that he had been murdered by his hosts. Shortly thereafter, Amal began to show signs of splintering.

When Ayatollah Ruhollah Khomeini rose to power in Iran after the 1979 Islamic revolution, Lebanon's Shiite population viewed his ascent as proof that Shiites could attain power. As a result, Amal's political power base was revived and expanded, and the movement's leaders called for other parties to join forces with it. Amal secured an alliance with the Lebanese Dawa Party, whose goals included "exerting influence from the inside and disseminat[ing] and entrenching the ideas of Islam among [Amal's] ranks."[8] Although Dawa and Amal united to form one party, Dawa members continued to maintain their separate identity, in part because Sheikh Muhammad Hussein Fadlallah, Dawa's spiritual leader, exerted immense influence over them.

Despite working closely with Amal, Tehran increasingly believed that the secular organization was ill-suited to the task of furthering Iranian goals. These sentiments came to a head with the creation of the Council of National Salvation (hereinafter CNS), which led to the end of Iranian support for Amal. In June 1982, following the Israeli invasion, President Sarkis of Lebanon called for the creation of this council in order to facilitate the formation of a functioning government. Iran opposed any cooperation with the CNS, however, on the grounds that it "symbolized the Western takeover of Lebanon and the perpetuation of the Zionist occupation of the country."[9] Despite Iran's objections, Nabih Berri, head of Amal, joined CNS in order to increase the body's Shiite representation. The heads of some of the country's other religious communities joined as well, including Bashir Gemayel, head of the Christian Lebanese Forces, and Walid Jumblatt, head of the Druze. Subsequently, Iran decided to form a new organization that would better represent its interests in Lebanon and export its radical Islamic ideology.

Toward that end, Iran called on members of Amal to disband and form a new party. Shortly after the creation of the CNS, the Lebanese Dawa Party, the Association of Muslim Clerics of Jabal Amel, and the Family of Brotherhood split from Amal and formed Amal al-Islami, or Islamic Amal. This new group, which received military, financial, and spiritual support from Iran, eventually came to be known as Hizballah.[10]

The name Hizballah, which means "Party of God," originates from the Quranic verse that states, "The party of Allah, they are the victorious."[11] Initially, the group was headed by Iraqi-educated Lebanese clerics such as Sheikh Subhi al-Tufayli (who would become Hizballah's first secretary-general) and Sheikh Abbas Musawi (Hizballah's second secretary-general), who pledged their support to Khomeini and to the creation of an Islamic republic in Lebanon.[12] In return, Iran sent a reported 1,500 to 5,000 Revolutionary Guards to assist Hizballah, along with arms, military hardware, tens of millions of dollars, and Islamic teachers.[13]

TARGETING U.S. INTERESTS FROM THE START

While Hizballah was in this nascent state, the Lebanese government asked President Ronald Reagan to send peacekeepers to assist in the forcible eviction of the PLO from Lebanon. Reagan agreed to send 800 U.S. Marines as part of a multinational peacekeeping force that included an equal number of Italian and French troops. The mission did not go as planned. Beginning in March 1983, a series of attacks was launched against the peacekeeping forces. On April 18, a suicide bomber drove a truck loaded with explosives into the U.S. embassy in Beirut, killing sixty-one people, including seventeen Americans.[14] The most significant attack, however, took place on October 23, when a suicide truck bomb destroyed the U.S. Marine barracks in the capital, killing 241 Americans. On the same day, twenty-three people were killed and more than 100 were wounded in an attack on the French contingent of the peacekeeping mission.[15]

A previously unknown organization named Islamic Jihad claimed responsibility for these attacks. Yet Sheikh Fadlallah, now widely regarded as Hizballah's spiritual leader, reportedly issued the *fatwa* (religious edict) sanctioning the bombings. Indeed, as information has emerged over the years, it has become increasingly apparent that Islamic Jihad and the nascent Hizballah organization were one and the same. Not surprisingly, Hizballah has repeatedly denied those charges.

As a result of the attacks, the multinational peacekeeping efforts were abandoned in March 1984. Subsequently, Hizballah pursued a strategy of kidnappings, bombings, terror tactics, and hijackings against civilians, military targets, and U.S. government officials throughout the 1980s.

The organization first announced its existence and elucidated its identity and goals in February 1985, when spokesman Sheikh Ibrahim al-Amin presented the party's first public message in a manifesto titled "The Open Letter That Hizballah Addressed to the Oppressed of Lebanon and the World."[16] The letter included the following statement:

> We are Hizballah....We are the sons of the *umma* [community of believers]....We obey the orders of one leader, wise and just, that of our tutor and *faqih* [jurist] who fulfills all the necessary conditions: Ruhollah Musawi Khomeini.[17]

The letter also depicted the United States as an arrogant superpower. One of Hizballah's declared aims was to

> tear out [America's] very roots, its primary roots....Our determination to fight the U.S. is solid....America, its Atlantic Pact allies, and the Zionist entity in the holy land of Palestine attacked us and continue to do so without respite. Their aim is to make us eat dust continually.

In addition to the United States, Hizballah named its enemies as "the Phalanges,[18] Israel, [and] France."

The manifesto also laid out Hizballah's main goals:

- Expel the Americans, the French, and their allies from Lebanon.
- Create an Islamic republic in Lebanon.
- Bring the Christian Phalanges to justice for their crimes.
- Encourage Christians to embrace Islam.
- Destroy Israel.

In attempting to fulfill these goals, Hizballah is estimated to have killed more than 300 individuals during the first ten years of its existence, in addition to the hundreds who died in the previously mentioned 1983 suicide attacks in Beirut.[19] Between 1982 and 1985 alone, Hizballah was responsible for at least thirty suicide bombings that were "dispatched in cars, suitcases, and even, on one occasion, by donkey."[20] Aside from kidnapping thousands of Lebanese, Hizballah reportedly abducted eighty-seven Westerners, including seventeen Americans, fourteen Britons, fifteen French, seven Swiss, and seven West Germans. At least ten Hizballah kidnapping victims perished in captivity during the 1980s; some were murdered, while others died from illnesses after being denied adequate medical attention.[21]

Hizballah was effective in pursuing its violent objectives against U.S. and other interests in large part due to the backing it received (and continues to receive) from Iran and Syria. From the party's inception, Iran has trained Hizballah operatives and provided them with various forms of assistance. Syria began actively supporting the organization in 1989, believing that it could use Hizballah for its own ends. According to one analyst,

> For Syria, Hizballah's greatest asset was (and is) military. Through Hizballah, Syria can wage a proxy war against Israelis in the occupied south....At the same time, Hizballah enables Syria to support an authentic Lebanese resistance movement.[22]

Although Hizballah's freedom of movement in Lebanon has depended on the occupying Syrian regime, the party has taken its ideological cues from Iran. As one frequently heard Lebanese proverb puts it, "Hizballah's brain is with Syria, but its heart lies with Iran."

EXPANDING POLITICAL AND INTERNATIONAL ACTIVITY

After fifteen years of war and 150,000 dead, Lebanon's civil war ended at the close of the 1980s, and the country's leaders signed the Taif Accord on October 22, 1989. Among the accord's provisions was a call for all militias to be dismantled. Hizballah, however, was exempted from this provision for a number of reasons. First, the group served the interests of the Lebanese government by fighting the Israeli occupation of southern Lebanon. Second, Syria hoped to use Hizballah as a lever for ousting Israel from the Golan Heights. Third, Iran wanted to preserve the group's status in order to maintain a measure of influence in the eastern Mediterranean.

The signing of the Taif Accord also led to changes in Hizballah's stance toward politics. Throughout the 1980s, Hizballah's leadership had refused to participate in Lebanon's political framework, believing that doing so would be counterproductive to their goal of creating an Islamic republic in Iran's image. After the Taif Accord was signed, however, Syria and Iran pressured Hizballah into entering the political arena. In Lebanon's 1992 parliamentary elections, the first to take place after two decades of war, Hizballah secured eight of the 128 seats in the legislature.[23] In the 1996 elections, Hizballah secured seven seats.[24] In the 2000 elections that followed Israel's withdrawal from Lebanon, Hizballah secured twelve seats.[25]

Some analysts have suggested that playing an active role in government would limit Hizballah's power to some degree and eventually coerce the group into transforming itself from a terrorist organization into a strictly sociopolitical organization. For example, one analyst maintained that Hizballah "has gradually lost its extremist edge in favor of pragmatism."[26] This assessment does not provide the full story, however. Even today, Hizballah refuses to accept positions in the Lebanese cabinet because doing so would require it to make concessions regarding its self-proclaimed "right of resistance" against Israel, the United States, and secular, pluralistic Lebanese governance. According to one historian, the organization's participation in the electoral process has given the party "a convenient, legitimate platform for working against the regime and undermining the Taif structure without fighting them."[27]

To be sure, Hizballah has created an impressive social base by setting up an array of public services, including schools, mosques, clinics, hospitals, community centers, and public assistance facilities. Doctors working in Hizballah's hospitals report that Muslims and Christians alike use these facilities. In addition, Hizballah's engineering and construction companies have "been quick to lend material support and expertise to those whose homes have been damaged or destroyed, whether by Israeli attacks or as a result of internecine clashes within Lebanon."[28] Such activity has enhanced Hizballah's standing among all religious denominations in Lebanon.

This "kinder, gentler" side of Hizballah has been used to bolster the party's membership and to increase popular support for its anti-Israeli activities. As the organization's previously mentioned inaugural manifesto stated, "Our struggle will end only when this [Zionist] entity is obliterated. We recognize no treaty with it, no cease fire, and no peace agreements, whether separate or consolidated."[29] Accordingly, fighting between Israel and Hizballah has occurred continually since the 1980s. In the early 1990s, Israel made a strategic decision to initiate a campaign to remove Hizballah from southern Lebanon. In February 1992, after weeks of fighting, Israel assassinated Hizballah secretary-general Sheikh Abbas Musawi, killing his wife, child, and five bodyguards in the process.[30] At the time, Musawi was the mastermind behind Hizballah's military operations, and Israel believed that assassinating him would lead to a significant drop in guerrilla activity. Musawi's death had the opposite effect, however. Soon after the assassination, Hizballah's newly elected secretary-general, Sheikh Hassan Nasrallah, vowed revenge.[31]

Hizballah's immediate response did not unfold in Israel or Lebanon, but rather in Argentina. In March 1992, a Hizballah suicide bomber attacked the Israeli embassy in Buenos Aires, killing thirty and injuring more than 250. True to its modus operandi, Hizballah did not claim responsibility for the bombing. Instead, a group named Islamic Jihad took credit in the name of "the martyr child of Hussein" (i.e., Musawi's son).[32]

Other Hizballah terrorist attacks against international targets followed. On July 18, 1994, terrorists bombed the Jewish cultural center in Buenos Aires, killing ninety-five people.[33] A group calling itself Ansar Allah issued a press release claiming responsibility for the attack. Security experts doubted Ansar's ability to carry out the bombing, however; they believed it was the work of Hizballah.[34] Similarly, on July 26, 1994, Hizballah operatives carried out two bomb attacks in London, against the Israeli embassy and the headquarters of a Jewish charity.[35]

Although Hizballah has repeatedly denied involvement in any of these attacks, U.S., Israeli, and Argentinean officials have linked the group to the Buenos Aires bombings. Hizballah has long used the South American "Triple Frontier" area as a base for planning terrorist activity. Located near the meeting point of Argentina, Brazil, and Paraguay, this area is a center of drug transactions and contraband smuggling. Argentinean authorities have concluded that Hizballah cells headquartered in the Triple Frontier carried out the 1992 and 1994 bombings in Buenos Aires.[36] Moreover, according to Argentinean security sources, Iran provided local logistical support for the bombings.[37] In March 2003, Argentinean judge Juan José Galeano issued arrest warrants against four Iranian officials for their involvement.[38]

The Argentina bombings were indicative of the expansion in Hizballah's worldwide operational capabilities during the 1990s. These and other attacks also made Imad Mughniyeh, the reported head of Hizballah's "external security apparatus" (the wing responsible for international activities), the focus of increased attention from Western intelligence. Mughniyeh is on the FBI's Most Wanted Terrorists list for his suspected involvement in several terrorist activities, including the aforementioned U.S. embassy and Marine barracks attacks in Beirut and the 1985 hijacking of TWA Flight 847. The U.S. Department of Justice is now offering $25 million for information leading to his arrest— the same amount offered for Osama bin Laden.[39] Mughniyeh has reportedly established networks in South America, the United States, Europe, and West Africa, in addition to serving as a liaison between Hizballah, Hamas, Palestinian Islamic Jihad, al-Qaeda, and other terrorist organizations.

In light of these and other far-reaching activities, some have also linked Hizballah to the 1996 attack on the Khobar Towers U.S. military complex in Saudi Arabia.[40] According to a U.S. government report, that attack may even have involved some degree of cooperation between Hizballah and al-Qaeda, given the past links between the two organizations.[41]

Avi Jorisch

RENEWED FOCUS ON ISRAEL

The mid-1990s saw the Hizballah-Israeli conflict play out with renewed intensity inside Lebanon, marked by a string of attacks, counterattacks, and semi-official truces. In 1993, after intense fighting between Israeli and Hizballah forces, Israel launched Operation Accountability, during which hundreds of thousands of Lebanese fled to Beirut as Israeli forces shelled Shiite villages in the south. Israel had hoped to pressure the Lebanese and Syrian governments into weakening Hizballah. This outcome did not come to pass, however, and Israel and Hizballah were forced to reach an understanding: Israel would not attack Lebanese civilians or Hizballah targets located in civilian areas, and Hizballah would not attack northern Israel.[42]

The truce did not last for long; fighting between the two sides broke out again in 1994, when Israel attacked a known Hizballah training camp in Ain Dardara. In general, Hizballah activity during this period served to establish a "balance of terror against Israel, which, alongside [Israel's] reluctance to bring too much pressure on Beirut lest talks with Damascus be slowed, in effect handicapped Israel."[43] Indeed, Israeli-Syrian peace talks had been conducted on and off throughout the 1990s. When progress slowed on the peace track, however, Syria often tried to wrangle concessions from Israel by giving Hizballah the green light to attack Israel's northern border.

Fighting in Lebanon intensified again in April 1996, when Israel launched Operation Grapes of Wrath. At one point during that operation, 107 Shiite civilians were killed when Israel inadvertently shelled a UN camp near Qana. By the operation's end, however, Hizballah and Israel had hammered out yet another informal agreement.

Overall, the events of the previous two decades had taken a heavy toll on both the Israeli and Lebanese public. Israel had invaded Lebanon in order to secure its northern border from PLO guerrilla attacks. But when the PLO was ejected in the early 1980s, Hizballah had taken the organization's place and assumed its guerrilla tactics. Israel was thus unable to find a viable exit strategy that would protect Israeli citizens in the north.

It was against this background—and shortly after an incident in which two Israeli military helicopters collided over southern Lebanon in February 1997, killing dozens of soldiers—that four Israeli mothers of fallen soldiers began demonstrating against Israel's presence in Lebanon. They subsequently formed a popular movement called the Four Mothers, which gained increasing traction by calling for withdrawal from a war that many in Israel compared with America's war in Vietnam. Approximately 1,500 Israeli soldiers died during the entire eighteen-year occupation of Lebanon, and, by the late 1990s, the Israeli public was no longer willing to accept the death toll.[44]

Upon being elected prime minister in July 1999, Ehud Barak announced his intention to withdraw the Israeli military from Lebanon. Barak hoped to begin this redeployment in the framework of peace negotiations, but was rebuffed by both Beirut and Damascus. Despite the security risks that were to inevitably follow, Barak went ahead with the withdrawal on May 25, 2000, thus ending Israel's occupation of Lebanon. This led many to believe that Hizballah had defeated Israel, and the party's reputation consequently soared throughout the entire Arab world.

Before the withdrawal, Hizballah had maintained that it would continue its militant operations if Israel were to retain even "one inch of Lebanese land." Indeed, since the withdrawal, Hizballah has engaged in a broadly defined border dispute with Israel over a small strip of land in an area called the Shebaa Farms, a twenty-five-square-kilometer stretch of cropland in the Golan Heights (captured by Israel during the 1967 war). This agricultural area, formerly farmed by Sunni residents of the nearby Lebanese village of Shebaa, is located on the border between Syria and Lebanon.

The Israeli government's stated position is that Israel has withdrawn fully from Lebanon. On July 24, 2001, the UN confirmed that Israeli authorities had "removed all violations of the line of withdrawal" and were fully compliant with UN Security Council Resolution 425.[45] The UN's demarcation of this line identified a border "based on the best available cartographic and other documentary evidence available." Yet UN secretary-general Kofi Annan has repeatedly emphasized that Resolution 425 refers only to the border that existed when Israel invaded Lebanon in 1978, not to the internationally recognized border of 1949. Such constructive ambiguity has led to an intolerable situation: Israel claims that it has pulled out of Lebanon in full, while Hizballah justifies continued attacks based on the ongoing international border dispute. This ambiguity has also allowed the Lebanese government to disregard its own constitution, which endorses the substance of Resolution 425.

IDEOLOGY OF RESISTANCE

Throughout its history, Hizballah has developed a unique ideology, much of which is based on militant Islam coupled with the philosophy of resistance. Militant Islam can be defined as

> a minority outgrowth of the faith that exudes a bitter hatred for Western ideas, including capitalism, individualism, and consumerism. It rejects the West and much that it has to offer (with the exception of weapons, medicines, and other useful technologies), seeking instead to implement a strict interpretation of the Qur'an...and Shari'a.[46]

Avi Jorisch

"Resistance" is an equally commanding theme in the discourse and ideology of Hizballah. It is one of the group's most powerfully articulated visions, and al-Manar Television—which calls itself "Qanat al-Muqawama," or "The Station of Resistance"— is the main vehicle for disseminating this ideology to a diverse audience in the Arab world. The meaning of the term is complex and provides a key to understanding Hizballah's popular appeal. Resistance, in the context of Hizballah, can be understood only if the words "oppression" and "occupation" immediately follow: that is, "resistance against oppression and occupation."

In contrast to the Sunni concept of Dar al-Harb (The abode of war) and Dar al-Islam (The abode of Islam), Hizballah focuses on oppressors *(mustakbiroun)* and oppressed *(mustad'afoun)*. The concept of oppression is emphasized both in speeches given by Hizballah officials and in statements made on al-Manar programs. The "oppressed" are not exclusively Muslims, but rather "those who were oppressed in the earth," whether socially, economically, politically, or culturally.[47] According to one analyst, much of Hizballah's terminology is "borrowed from Marxism and the Qur'an [and]…infused with a sense of moral dualism and millennialism in its division of mankind into good and evil forces."[48] By dividing the world into oppressors and oppressed, Hizballah justifies working with both Muslim (Sunni and Shiite alike) and non-Muslim groups. As a rule, Hizballah's litmus test for making this division is based on the group's attitude toward Zionism and the West—the United States in particular.

Hizballah's list of enemies, as elucidated by al-Manar programming, is best understood as three concentric circles. The innermost circle includes the "Zionist entity" and the United States. Indeed, Hizballah regards Israel's very existence as an act of terrorism. Therefore, it believes that most, if not all, acts of violence against Israel are legitimate. As Nayef Krayem, al-Manar's general manager and chairman of the board, put it, "There is no act of resistance that can be classified as terrorism.…Civilians and military are both occupiers and, therefore, both are legitimate targets."[49] Moreover, Hizballah considers all land west of the Jordan River to be occupied and consequently demands the dismantling of what it calls the "Zionist entity." The group believes that Israel's existence is based on a racist, colonialist ideology that embodies Western expansion into Muslim lands. Such expansion is in turn viewed as an attempt to establish Western territorial influence from the Nile to the Euphrates and to wreak havoc on the lives of Arabs and Muslims. In particular, Hizballah considers U.S. foreign policy to be hegemonic and oppressive. As evidence for this assertion, it cites America's role as the primary economic backer of the embodiment of state terrorism, Israel.

The second circle of Hizballah's enemies includes any country that occupies land illegally and oppresses the rightful inhabitants of that land. Prominent examples include Britain (vis-à-vis its policy toward Northern Ireland) and India (vis-à-vis its policy toward Kashmir).

The third circle comprises regimes that are subservient to the West, particularly to the United States. This category includes countries in the European Union. From Hizballah's perspective, the oppressed of the earth are victims of the countries in these three categories. Accordingly, the organization urges all of its "allies" to unite and "form a common 'international front' to fight oppression."[50]

Although al-Manar does not actually carry out acts of terrorism against Hizballah's various enemies, it believes its job is to "inspire them."[51] Nayef Krayem described the station's role as follows: "We do not create these acts, but we do support any resistance acts through our media. We cover and promote any act of resistance on our programming." From Krayem's—and Hizballah's—point of view, any such act "is actually an act against terrorism."

NOTES

1.   Secretary of State Madeleine Albright approved the FTO designation for Hizballah and twenty-nine other groups in October 1997. See U.S. Department of State, "Fact Sheet: Foreign Terrorist Organizations," August 15, 2002. Available online (www.state.gov/coalition/cr/fs/12713.htm).

2.   See U.S. Department of the Treasury, Office of Foreign Assets Control, "Terrorism: What You Need to Know about U.S. Sanctions" (n.d.). Available online (www.treasury.gov/offices/eotffc/ofac/sanctions/t11ter.pdf).

3.   See the text of the International Emergency Economic Powers Act, available online (www.treas.gov/offices/eotffc/ofac/legal/statutes/ieepa.pdf). In addition, U.S. Code makes it illegal to "knowingly provide material support or resources to a Foreign Terrorist Organization." U.S. Code, Title 18, Part I, Chap. 113-B, Sec. 2339-B.

4.   Neil MacFarquhar, "Hezbollah Becomes Potent Anti-U.S. Force," *New York Times,* December 24, 2002.

5.   Habib Malik, *Between Damascus and Jerusalem: Lebanon and Middle East Peace* (Washington, D.C.: The Washington Institute for Near East Policy, 2000).

6.   Marilyn Raschka, "Uneasy Coexistence: A Look inside Israeli-Occupied Lebanon," *Washington Report on Middle East Affairs* (June 1995), p. 57. Available online (www.washington-report.org/backissues/0695/9506051.htm). From 1982 to 1985, Israel controlled a much larger swath of Lebanese territory. In 1985, Israel withdrew from part of this area, maintaining control over the aforementioned 410-square-mile zone until 2000.

7.   "Amal" is both an acronym for "Afwaj al-Muqawamat al-Lubnaniya" (Lebanese resistance detachments) and an Arabic word meaning "hope."

8. Shimon Shapira, "The Origins of Hizbollah," *Jerusalem Quarterly*, no. 46 (Spring 1988), p. 118.

9. Ibid., p. 121.

10. Ibid. See also Martin Kramer, "The Moral Logic of Hizballah," in Walter Reich (ed.), *Origins of Terrorism: Psychologies, Ideologies, Theologies, States of Mind* (London: Cambridge University Press, 1990), pp. 131–157. See also Eyal Zisser, "Hizballah in Lebanon: At the Crossroads," *Middle East Review of International Affairs (MERIA) 1*, no. 3 (1997), p. 6. Available online (www.biu.ac.il/SOC/besa/meria/journal/1997/issue3/jv1n3a1.html).

11. The Quran, "The Table" (Al-ma'idah), verse 56. See also M. M. Pickthal, *The Meaning of the Glorious Qu'ran* (Flushing, N.Y.: Asia Book Corporation of America, 1979).

12. Shapira, "The Origins of Hizbollah," pp. 125–126.

13. Zisser, "Hizballah in Lebanon: At the Crossroads." See also Hala Jaber, *Hezbollah: Born with a Vengeance* (New York: Columbia University Press, 1997), pp. 107–108.

14. Jack Redden, untitled report, United Press International, April 22, 1983.

15. Wadie Kirolos, untitled report, United Press International, October 24, 1983.

16. Originally *Nass al-Risalat al-Maftouha allati wajahaha Hizbollah ila al-Mustad'afin fi Lubnan wa al-Alam.* The manifesto was published in the Lebanese daily al-Safir on February 16, 1985.

17. "An Open Letter: The Hizballah Program," International Policy Institute for Counter-Terrorism (n.d.). Available online (www.ict.org.il/Articles/Hiz_letter.htm). This webpage presents an expanded version of an English translation of the Hizballah manifesto originally provided in the *Jerusalem Quarterly*, no. 48 (Fall 1988).

18. Members of the Phalanges, a Lebanese Christian militia, were responsible for the September 1982 massacres in the Palestinian refugee camps of Sabra and Shatila.

19. Magnus Ranstorp, *Hizb'Allah in Lebanon: The Politics of the Western Hostage Crisis* (New York: St. Martin's Press, 1996), p. 60.

20. Jaber, *Hezbollah: Born with a Vengeance,* p. 76.

21. Ibid., p. 113.

22. Graham Usher, "Hizballah, Syria, and the Lebanese Elections," *Journal of Palestine Studies 26,* no. 2 (Winter 1997), p. 62.

23. Hizballah's parliamentary bloc was known as "Kutlat al-Wafa li al-Muqawama" (Loyalty to the resistance). Hizballah was not the only fundamentalist Muslim organization to secure seats in the legislature. Al-Jamaat al-Islamiya (The Islamic group) secured three seats, while Jamiyat al-Mashari al-Khayriyat al-Islamiya (The Islamic society of philanthropic protests) secured one. See A. Nizar Hamzeh, "Lebanon's Hizbullah: From Islamic Revolution to Parliamentary Accommodation," *Third World Quarterly* 14, no. 2 (1993); available online (http://almashriq.hiof.no/ddc/projects/pspa/hamzeh2.html). Hizballah was able to count on these four parliamentary seats during voting. For that reason, some analysts credit Hizballah with twelve seats in the 1992 elections. See, for example, Jaber, *Hezbollah: Born with a Vengeance,* p. 72, and Usher, "Hizballah, Syria, and the Lebanese Elections," pp. 59–60.

24. Hizballah was also able to claim the support of three other fundamentalist-held seats in parliament following this election. See Usher, "Hizballah, Syria, and the Lebanese Elections," pp. 59–60.

25. Dalal Saoud, "Hezbollah Boosts Presence in Lebanon Parliament," United Press International, September 4, 2000.

26. Nicholas Blanford, "Hezbullah Attacks Force Israel to Take a Hard Look at Lebanon," *Jane's Intelligence Review* 11, no. 4 (April 1999), pp. 32–37.

27. Zisser, "Hizballah in Lebanon: At the Crossroads."

28. Augustus Richard Norton, "Hizballah: From Radicalism to Pragmatism?" *Middle East Policy Council Journal* 5, no. 4 (January 1998). Available online (www.mepc.org/public_asp/journal_vol5/9801_norton.asp).

29. "An Open Letter: The Hizballah Program."

30. James Dorsey, "Lebanon: Israeli Attacks Intended to Settle Fate of Missing Flyer," Inter Press Service, February 19, 1992.

31. Mohammed Salam, "New Hezbollah Leader a Disciple of Iran's Revolution," Associated Press, February 18, 1992.

32. Ranstorp, *Hizb'Allah in Lebanon: The Politics of the Western Hostage Crisis,* p. 107.

33. Nayla W. Razzouk, "Muslim Group Claims Argentina Blast," United Press International, July 23, 1994.

34. Carl Anthony Wege, "Hizbollah Organization," *Studies in Conflict and Terrorism* 17, no. 2 (1994), pp. 151–164. Indeed, Hizballah has used the Ansar Allah alias elsewhere. Today, Ansar is recognized as a faction of Hizballah based in Ain al-Hilwa, a Palestinian refugee camp known for lawlessness and violence. Hashem Kassem, "Understanding the Significance of Ain al-Hilweh," *EastWest Record,* August 26, 2002. Available online (www.eastwestrecord.com/Get_Articles.asp?articleId=480).

35. "Scotland Yard Perplexed in Hunt for Antisemitic Bombers," Agence France Presse, July 28, 1994. See also U.S. Department of State, daily press briefing, July 29, 1994; available online (http://dosfan.lib.uic.edu/ERC/briefing/daily_briefings/1994/9407/940729db.html).

36. See Blanca Madani, "Hezbollah's Global Finance Network: The Triple Frontier," *Middle East Intelligence Bulletin* 4, no. 1 (January 2002). Available online (www.meib.org/articles/0201_l2.htm).

37. Anthony Faiola, "Argentina Links Iran to Terror Bombings; Blast at Israeli Embassy, Jewish Center Killed 110," *Washington Post,* May 21, 1998.

38. "Argentina Seeks Arrest of Iranian Diplomats in Its Worst Terror Attack," Agence France Presse, March 8, 2003.

39. Mughniyeh's profile on the FBI Most Wanted list is available online (www.fbi.gov/mostwant/terrorists/termugniyah.htm).

40. Isabel Kershner, "The Changing Colors of Imad Mughniya," *Jerusalem Report* (March 25, 2002), pp. 25–27.

41. National Commission on Terrorist Attacks upon the United States, "Overview of the Enemy," Staff Statement no. 15, presented at the commission's twelfth public hearing, June 16, 2004. Available online (www.9-11commission.gov/hearings/hearing12/staff_statement_15.pdf). The commission noted that the links between Hizballah and al-Qaeda transcended "the historical animosity between Shia and Sunni Muslims." For example, during the early 1990s, a contingent of representatives from al-Qaeda, a Sunni organization, met with Iranian officials. Subsequently, a small number of al-Qaeda operatives received training in Hizballah camps.

42. Zisser, "Hizballah in Lebanon: At the Crossroads."

43. Ibid.

44. Lisa Beyer, "Withdrawal Symptoms," *Time* (international edition) 155, no. 16 (April 24, 2000), p. 44.

45. See Kofi Annan, "Letter dated 24 July 2000 from the Secretary-General addressed to the President of the Security Council," UN Security Council (document S/2000/731). Available online (http://domino.un.org/UNISPAL.nsf/0/2e1e149a5c7c6b41852569b600724cff?OpenDocument).

46. Jonathan Schanzer, "At War with Whom? A Short History of Radical Islam," *Doublethink* (Spring 2002), p. 4. Available online (www.affdoublethink.com/pdfs/2002-2-spring.pdf).

47. The Quran, "The Stories" (Al-qasas), verse 5. See also Pickthal, *The Meaning of the Glorious Qu'ran.*

48. Amal Saad-Ghorayeb, *Hizbullah: Politics and Religion* (London: Pluto Press, 2002), p. 17.

49. Unless otherwise indicated, all quotes attributed to al-Manar and Hizballah personnel were obtained from the individuals in question during interviews conducted at the Beirut station on June 27–28, 2002. The titles attributed to these personnel represent the positions they held at the time of the interviews.

50. Ibrahim Musawi (al-Manar's English-language editor-in-chief), interview by author, al-Manar Television station, Beirut, June 27, 2002.

51. Interview granted to author on condition of anonymity, Art Graphic Department, al-Manar Television station, Beirut, June 27, 2002.

CHAPTER 2

HISTORY AND OPERATIONAL BACKGROUND OF AL-MANAR TELEVISION

Since beaming its first signal on June 3, 1991, al-Manar Television has served Hizballah as an effective propaganda weapon. Having expanded from a ramshackle local operation to a twenty-four-hour satellite station boasting global coverage (see video clip 1), al-Manar now plays a major role in helping Hizballah promote itself, advance its worldview, and preach resistance against the West. With continuous funding from Iran, the station has grown by leaps and bounds as it has gained credibility, viewers, and followers.

REFERENCE VIDEO CLIP
1

Al-Manar has also become an indispensable operational weapon to Hizballah. Indeed, while touring the station in Beirut and meeting with its board of directors on November 24, 2000, Hizballah secretary-general Sheikh Hassan Nasrallah praised al-Manar for its part in both supporting the Palestinian intifada and forcing the Israel Defense Forces (IDF) to withdraw from Lebanon.[1] Hizballah even distributed bumper stickers following the withdrawal that asserted, "Without al-Manar, victory would have been elusive."[2]

In 1992, Ali Dahir, al-Manar's first general manager, explained that Hizballah had established the station to "express the views of the oppressed…and advocate a mass media that respects Islamic morals and Muslim tradition." He continued, "The goal of our station is to show the facts, focus on our hostility and hate toward Israel and its racist government system, whose downfall we see as a fundamental principle of ours."[3] Similarly, Muhammad Afif Ahmed, the station's second general manager, asserted that al-Manar has belonged to Hizballah "culturally and politically" from its establishment.[4] Although the station registered as the Lebanese Media Group Company in 1997, it is operated by Hizballah members, reports directly to Hizballah officials, and takes its marching orders from Hassan Nasrallah's office.[5]

Avi Jorisch

Nayef Krayem, al-Manar's third general manager and chairman of the board,[6] asserted that the station is an arm of Hizballah's mass media efforts and is used to express the party's global outlook. According to him,

> Al-Manar gets its political support for the continuation of the channel from Hizballah. It gets money from the shareholders [who] are leaders in Hizballah.…[Al-Manar and Hizballah] breathe life into one another. Each provides the other with inspiration. Hizballah uses al-Manar to express its stands and its views, etc. Al-Manar, in turn, receives political support for its continuation.[7]

The station itself is strategically located in the poor, Shiite-controlled Harat Hurayk neighborhood in the southern suburbs of Beirut. This location belies the considerable funding that al-Manar has received since its inception. Unlike western Beirut, where clubs, alcohol, and Western culture abound, Harat Hurayk is conservative and strongly affiliated with Hizballah.

Housed in a high-tech six-story building, al-Manar appears to the casual observer like any other television station. It has newsrooms, reporters, studios, state-of-the-art editing suites, and television screens with feeds from the world's leading media. Staff members carefully monitor other television networks such as CNN, BBC, al-Jazeera, and various Israeli channels.

Upon closer examination, however, it is clear that al-Manar differs significantly from its counterparts. Armed Hizballah guards stand watch outside the station and check visitors' papers and belongings for security purposes. In the marble-floored lobby, two pictures are displayed showing al-Manar cameramen Bakr Haidar Ahmed and Behjet Dakroub, who were killed during Israeli military operations in July 1993.[8] Male employees dress in suits, but all of the women wear the traditional Islamic veil. Their dress contrasts sharply with that of other Lebanese television stations, which feature female news anchors wearing revealing clothing. The station also has an extensive library with thousands of carefully labeled al-Manar videotapes. According to Bilal Zaarour, the station's programming manager, the video collection is housed on one of the basement floors for fear of Israeli or U.S. attacks.[9] In fact, Zaarour asserted, al-Manar built "another base in case the station is bombed."

Al-Manar was launched by a small group of men who studied media in London during the mid-1980s.[10] According to Krayem and Zaarour, the station now employs approximately 300 workers of American, Egyptian, Jordanian, Lebanese, Moroccan, and Palestinian nationalities. Although employees are not required to be Hizballah members, former general manager Ahmed stated, "We prefer it all the same."[11] Indeed, most of the station's male reporters apparently served as guerrilla fighters before they joined al-Manar.[12] Al-Manar also "employs Palestinians who speak Hebrew and who were brought up in the 'occupied territories,' but who left or were expelled by Israel, to prepare and present Hizballah's Hebrew television programs."[13] These same individuals "have been managing the monitoring unit of Hizballah, which listens to the Zionist occupation army's communications." Moreover, many of al-Manar's Hebrew speakers are reportedly "veteran Hezbollah fighters who served time in Israeli or [Southern Lebanese Army] jails, where they learned the language."[14]

According to Zaarour, most of the station's employees are in their twenties or thirties and have learned their trade on the job. Many station officials have attended special training courses to enhance their political, social, educational, and technical backgrounds. Station officials also attend classes at colleges or institutes and sometimes even take courses over the internet in cooperation with international companies.[15] In 1997, the Lebanese press reported that al-Manar officials attended lectures and seminars on the workings of the Israeli Foreign Ministry and other Israeli agencies in order to help the station carry out a successful propaganda campaign. Station officials have also reportedly attended courses on world weather and sports news.[16] In addition, station journalists and technicians have upgraded their qualifications through training sessions with organizations such as Reuters and the Thomson Foundation (a company that specializes in media training).[17]

Although headquartered in Beirut, al-Manar has bureaus in Egypt, Iran, Jordan, and the United Arab Emirates (Dubai).[18] According to Ibrahim Musawi, editor-in-chief of the English news desk, the station plans to open a bureau in the United Kingdom in the near future. Al-Manar also has eight full-time correspondents in Lebanon and ten to sixteen abroad in places such as Belgium, France, Egypt, Iran, Iraq, Jordan, Kosovo, Kuwait, Morocco, the Palestinian territories, Russia, Sweden, Syria, Turkey, the United Arab Emirates, and the United States (see video clip 2).[19]

REFERENCE VIDEO CLIPS
2 and 3

In addition, al-Manar employs a number of special correspondents in the Palestinian territories and Iraq. Their placement enables the station to effectively cover breaking news; in fact, al-Manar is often the first station to break news on these two fronts. In some cases, for example, exclusive information about terrorist attacks is flashed at the bottom of the screen (e.g., see video clip 3).[20] According to Krayem, the station even employs freelancers when necessary (though it prefers to use its own staff).

Moreover, during the first few months of Operation Enduring Freedom in Afghanistan, al-Manar was able to show extensive coverage of the U.S. military operation. Only days after the September 11, 2001, attacks on the United States, the station dispatched its Tehran correspondent (also employed by Iranian Television) and a crew to southwestern Afghanistan. Another crew was sent to Islamabad, Pakistan. According to Krayem, al-Manar's Afghan presence cost $2,500 for each five-minute report, with the total bill running into the hundreds of thousands of dollars.[21] Similarly, during and after Operation Iraqi Freedom in spring 2003, al-Manar employed at least two correspondents to cover the conflict: one in Baghdad and one on the Iranian border.

Indeed, close coverage of military operations has long been a staple of al-Manar's news programming. Prior to Israel's withdrawal from Lebanon, the station was notorious for receiving significant portions of its news footage from camera crews wearing flak jackets and running alongside Hizballah guerrillas during attacks. Such cameramen were often in position in advance of guerrilla operations, thus demonstrating foreknowledge of the attacks and a high degree of cooperation with Hizballah's guerrilla units. Al-Manar often coordinated with Hizballah's "military media service" to ensure the safety of the cameramen and the best position from which to film attacks. Reportedly, both live footage of this sort and timely audiovisual material have often been sent to Beirut via a microwave dish.[22] This capability has given al-Manar immediate access to images of breaking stories. Haytham Tabesh, editor of the United Arab Emirates daily *al-Ittidad,* has called such operations "Resistance Media."[23]

FOUNDING AND HISTORY

Although most television stations in the Arab world today are state run, there are a few notable exceptions. Al-Manar is the only outlet of its kind in the region: a twenty-four-hour station that is run by a terrorist organization and used as a mouthpiece to disseminate propaganda and promote terrorist activity. As a result of extraordinary historical events, however, many regard al-Manar as a legitimate station that serves an important role in Lebanese society, just as they regard Hizballah as something other than a terrorist organization. In order to understand al-Manar, then, one must place it in the historical context of Lebanese media.

On May 28, 1959, La Compagnie Libanaise (CLT) became the first television station to broadcast within Lebanon and the first commercial station to broadcast in the Arab world.[24] Over time, additional stations began broadcasting in Lebanon. During the civil war that erupted in 1975, militias set up their own stations as tools aimed at winning the hearts and minds of constituents and foes. The absence of central authority during the war permitted these "illegal" stations to operate freely.

Once the war ended in 1989, Hizballah began to play a more active role in Lebanese politics (see chapter 1). Previously, the organization had not been interested in reaching out to the broader Lebanese body politic. Once Hizballah decided to integrate into the political scene, however, establishing a television station became an indispensable step in its efforts to be taken seriously.

The 1989 Taif Accord contained a clause that called for the reorganization of Lebanese media, and the government deemed the television industry to be part of this effort.[25] In November 1994, Lebanon passed a law subjecting all stations to government licensing. Public debate and even widespread protest ensued because station owners and members of the government opposition were skeptical of the new process and feared that nepotism would be the determining factor in licensing.

In September 1996, the government granted licenses to only five television stations.[26] These five stations were purportedly selected with Lebanon's broad demographic landscape in mind.[27] The stations chosen were:

- Tele-Liban, the government's official station;
- Lebanese Broadcasting Company International (LBCI), representing Maronite Christians;[28]
- Future Television (al-Mustaqbal), owned by Prime Minister Rafiq Hariri and representing Sunnis;
- Murr Television, owned by the family of former interior minister Michel al-Murr and representing Greek Orthodox Christians; and
- the National Broadcasting Network, owned by the family and supporters of the Speaker of the House in the Lebanese parliament (Nabih Berri, who is also head of the Amal Party) and representing Lebanese Shiites.

At the same time, approximately fifty stations were ordered closed. The government argued that the reduction was necessary for "technical" reasons and voiced its "determination to put an end to years of media anarchy and partisan propaganda which emerged during the war."[29]

As a result of these decisions, the government faced widespread criticism. Many believed that the licensing choices were based on political and sectarian considerations rather than professional standards. Moreover, a number of the stations that did not receive a license, including al-Manar, refused to stop broadcasting.[30] The government threatened these stations, in some cases even using force to carry out the law. Several stations appealed the government's decision, but only four of them were granted licenses, including al-Manar. On September 18, 1996, at the request of Syrian president Hafiz al-Asad, the Lebanese cabinet decided to grant al-Manar an operating license, which it finally received in July 1997.[31]

Nayef Krayem maintained that al-Manar received permission to continue broadcasting after putting "pressure on parliament and utilizing outside sources, which also put pressure on the government." This "outside pressure" entailed sending a delegation to Damascus to secure permission from al-Asad for continued al-Manar programming.[32] That measure was yet another demonstration of Syria's control over Lebanon and its ability to influence the outcome of major political decisionmaking. Hizballah was the only Lebanese militia permitted to remain in existence under the Taif Accord, largely in order to fulfill Damascus and Beirut's goal of removing Israel from southern Lebanon and the Golan Heights. Al-Manar was given permission to continue operating because it was regarded as an important tool in achieving those goals.

During the early 1990s, the Arab world, including Lebanon, witnessed a significant increase in satellite broadcasting. The first Lebanese television station to realize the potential of this new market was Future Television, which established Future International SAT in October 1994.[33] LBCI followed shortly thereafter, launching LBCSAT in 1996.[34] Following the success of those stations, the Lebanese government eventually launched its own satellite channel, Tele-Liban Satellite.

Looking both to compete with other Lebanese stations and to cultivate an international audience, al-Manar publicly announced its intention to launch a satellite channel on March 9, 2000. Soon thereafter, Muhammad Ra'd, a Hizballah member of parliament and al-Manar's largest shareholder, officially submitted Hizballah's request to the minister of transmission.[35] The Council of Ministers approved the request in April 2000.[36] According to Krayem, although the launch was originally set for July 2000, Hizballah decided to move up the date to coincide with the May 25 Israeli withdrawal from southern Lebanon.[37] The symbolism was not lost on al-Manar's viewers or Middle East analysts; the launching of al-Manar's satellite channel came to signify freedom from Israeli occupation.

The success of Lebanon's pioneering satellite stations encouraged two other stations to launch satellite programming: Murr TV began satellite transmission in November 2000,[38] and New TV followed in October 2001.[39] On September 5, 2002, however, Lebanese authorities closed down Murr TV, charging it with "violating an election law prohibiting propaganda."[40]

In fact, the station was closed because of its vehement opposition to the Syrian occupation of Lebanon. In late October 2002, the Lebanese courts turned down an appeal to reopen the station.[41] The fate of Murr TV shows that Syria and Lebanon engage in political censorship when it suits their purposes. The fact that al-Manar has continued to operate is a clear sign that the station has full political approval from Damascus and Beirut, thus legitimizing Hizballah and its message of hate.

GOALS AND TARGET AUDIENCE

Al-Manar was created to spread propaganda. Although the station's programming may appear similar to what other Arab stations offer, it is certainly not objective. According to al-Manar's main website (www.manartv.com),[42] the station's primary goal is to wage "effective psychological warfare against the Zionist enemy." Station officials also admit that al-Manar exists to promote Hizballah's image in Lebanon and beyond and to spread the party's Islamic revolutionary worldview. The station is only the latest addition to Hizballah's mass media organ. According to Krayem, Hizballah also uses *al-Intiqad* newspaper (founded in 1982 and formerly known as *al-Ahd*) and al-Nur radio (founded in 1988 and currently broadcast on Nile SAT and on various frequencies throughout the Middle East) to disseminate propaganda (see video clips 4 and 5).[43]

REFERENCE VIDEO CLIPS
4 and 5

With relatively primitive equipment that cost as little as "a few million dollars," al-Manar's initial broadcast signal in 1992 barely reached Beirut's southern suburbs.[44] Today, al-Manar uses some of the most advanced broadcasting equipment in Lebanon (much of which it purchased from Sony), and its terrestrial signal is able to reach well beyond the country's borders.[45] Similarly, starting with only a handful of dedicated employees in May 1991, the station began advertising additional positions in the Lebanese press shortly after launching its first signal.[46] Within a year, the number of employees had reached 150;[47] as mentioned previously, its current level is 300.

Alongside this physical growth, al-Manar has gradually expanded the amount and types of programming it offers in order to increase both Hizballah's and its own popularity among the Lebanese people. Initially, its broadcasting lasted only five hours per day. Shortly before the 1992 elections, however, al-Manar began broadcasting regular news bulletins in the hope of disseminating Hizballah's message to more people and thus securing more parliamentary seats for the party.[48] In 1993, the station increased its regular coverage to seven hours per day and extended its signal to the southern part of the Bekaa Valley. While preparing for the 1996 parliamentary elections, Hizballah erected additional antennas in northern Lebanon and throughout the Mount Lebanon range to expand its audience and secure more votes. By the time the elections took place, al-Manar could be viewed throughout Lebanon, western Syria, and northern Israel. Broadcasting increased to twelve hours daily in 1998 and to eighteen hours in 2000.

When al-Manar launched its satellite channel in May 2000, transmission lasted three hours per day. By December 2000, the station had begun round-the-clock programming—the result of a direct order from Hizballah leader Hassan Nasrallah.[49] Initially, the management of ArabSat—one of the leading satellite companies in the Arab world—was apprehensive about granting space to al-Manar on its satellite package because of Hizballah's Shiite sectarian agenda. After negotiations, the two organizations agreed that, as a precondition for transmission, al-Manar's satellite channel would not advocate any such sectarian agenda. Sheikh Nasir al-Akhdar, al-Manar's programming director at the time, asserted that the station was "not thinking in terms of being a spokesman for the Shi'i sect."[50]

In this manner, al-Manar began vying for a new target audience: the pan-Arab and Islamic world. As a result, al-Manar's terrestrial and satellite programming differ slightly. Sectarian programming is broadcast terrestrially for local constituents, whereas more diverse material is broadcast on the satellite network for viewers worldwide.

PRIMARY AUDIENCE

Throughout the 1990s, al-Manar's traditional target audience was the Lebanese public, which was only natural given that the station's signal reached only slightly beyond the country's borders. Consequently, programming focused on the Israeli occupation of Lebanon and on domestic issues. The launch of satellite programming meant a more global agenda was necessary, however. Al-Manar began changing its programming to target the wider Arab world and, to a lesser extent, Israelis (both Jewish and Arab; see "Secondary Audience" section below). In fact, the station began to regard itself as the superstation of Muslims and Arabs worldwide, going so far as to advertise itself as "Qanat al-Arab wa al-Muslimin," or "The Station of Arabs and Muslims" (see video clip 6).

REFERENCE VIDEO CLIP
6

As Nayef Krayem maintained, the station aspired to give viewers a feeling that they "belong to something greater than themselves—something that is pan-human, pan-Muslim, and pan-Arab." Al-Manar also began to project itself as a guardian of Islamic values, which gave it credibility in Muslim religious circles.

REFERENCE VIDEO CLIP 7

In targeting a worldwide pan-Arab audience, Hizballah began by highlighting the Palestinian cause and the perceived Israeli occupation of all land west of the Jordan River. Although Hizballah's anti-American bent still colored much of al-Manar's programming, the Israeli-Palestinian issue became the station's focal point following Israel's withdrawal from Lebanon and the outbreak of the Palestinian intifada in September 2000 (see video clip 7). The station offered a number of ideological justifications for this change in focus:

- Lebanon borders what Hizballah refers to as "1948 Palestine." As Krayem asserted, "Occupation is not in the Philippines but right next door."
- From al-Manar's perspective, "Palestinians are oppressed Muslims and Christians"— a cornerstone of Hizballah's ideology (see chapter 1).
- Because Palestinians have helped Hizballah in its battle against Israel, Hizballah must offer its services in kind.
- Palestinians and Lebanese share a mutual enemy: Israel. As Farah Nour al-Din, one of al-Manar's news editors, put it, the "enemy is one."[51]

Indeed, al-Manar soon began to use images of the Israeli-Palestinian conflict as weapons of war. As early as October 2000, the station's programming amounted to a "drum beat of carefully selected, dramatically composed, one-sided visual accounts of West Bank and Gaza violence beamed across Lebanon and, via satellite, to a vast regional audience, transmissions which incite the Arab world to mobilize popular support for the Palestinian cause."[52] Al-Manar transmitted—and continues to transmit—this powerful visual message as a means of taking the Arab world to task for not doing enough for the Palestinians. As Krayem noted,

> The Arab world should take care of this problem and give it more attention....We have an important role to play in pushing people to go out and demonstrate on behalf of the Palestinians and support their cause....Affecting the Palestinians is our main role....We are here to support Palestinian resistance and their cause.

REFERENCE VIDEO CLIPS 8 and 9

Similarly, Nasrallah has repeatedly called for greater regional unity and support of the Palestinian cause: "The streets should not be quiet; demonstrations should fill the streets each day in the Arab world" (see video clips 8 and 9).[53]

Al-Manar's strong identification with the Palestinian cause was highlighted in December 2001 following the destruction of Palestinian Television facilities by Israeli forces. Shortly after that incident, al-Manar carried the Palestinian Television logo for two days in place of its own.[54] Station officials declared that this step was taken within the framework of "solidarity with an Arab media organ."[55]

When Operation Iraqi Freedom was launched in 2003, however, al-Manar again altered its programming in order to appeal to a broader pan-Arab audience. Although the station continued its efforts on the Israeli-Palestinian front, it also rested its sights on the U.S. invasion and occupation of Iraq (see chapter 3). During the war, al-Manar began directing most of its energy to covering the conflict and calling for violent acts against Americans in the region. Primetime programming included talk shows with titles such as *Hard on the Heels of the Event* (focusing on U.S. military operations) and *American Aggression.* Music and propaganda videos directed their message of hate against U.S. leaders and the war itself, showing the most grotesque images available. Indeed, al-Manar's anti-American message became quite similar to its anti-Israel vitriol, often employing identical language and images (e.g., see video clip 10).

REFERENCE VIDEO CLIP
10

SECONDARY AUDIENCE

Perhaps surprisingly, al-Manar eventually began to target Israeli Jews and Arabs as its secondary audience. As early as 1996, the station broadcast propaganda videos in Hebrew that addressed the Israeli public, warning of the dangers of remaining in Lebanon.[56] According to *al-Istiqlal,* a weekly paper published by Palestinian Islamic Jihad (PIJ), Hizballah launched this particular campaign in an effort to "undermine the morale of the Zionist occupation forces… and sow a rift among the Zionists."[57] This type of propaganda has continued, and the station now airs videos that specifically target Russian- and English-speaking segments of Israeli society.[58]

Since its inception, al-Manar's Hebrew campaign has been directed at three segments of the Jewish population: the IDF, Israeli civilians, and Israeli political analysts. Regarding the Israeli military, al-Manar has long pursued a policy of undermining "the morale of the IDF." For example, the station publicly maintained that its media coverage caused IDF soldiers in Lebanon to desert their posts, increased the number of IDF suicide attempts, and fostered a rise in drug abuse among the troops.[59] Following Israel's withdrawal from Lebanon, al-Manar began to target IDF soldiers serving in the Shebaa Farms area.

In addition, by showing "live video coverage of every operation carried out," al-Manar officials hoped that Israelis would see the death of fellow citizens in real-time coverage and, presumably, react with fear.[60] Yet some analysts suggest that al-Manar's effect on Jewish Israelis may not be as great as station officials would like. Reuven Paz, academic director at the International Policy Institute for Counter-Terrorism, maintained that al-Manar's transmissions are frequently cited by the Israeli media, which broadcasts images from Hizballah operations. Paz acknowledged that such broadcasting "likely does have some effect in Israel."[61] Because Israel's cable packages do not offer al-Manar, however, the only Israeli Jews who have direct access to the station's programming are those who subscribe to ArabSat, those who are area experts, and those who are residents of northern Israel (which is close enough to the Lebanese border to receive al-Manar's terrestrial signal by antenna).[62] This already small potential audience is further limited to Israeli Jews who understand Arabic.

Although al-Manar is cognizant of its failure to reach most Israelis, it is also keenly aware that Israel's political and military analysts do watch the station. According to Nayef Krayem, such analysts "watch our programming and comment on it, publish it in their papers, and show the coverage on their channels." From this perspective, he maintained, al-Manar programming—especially its Hebrew videos—played a "very sensitive and important role" in forcing Israel to withdraw from Lebanon. By taping and airing resistance operations against the IDF and by repeatedly showing Hizballah's "success" in causing Israeli fatalities and casualties, al-Manar believed that it could eventually penetrate the Israeli psyche and destroy the country's morale, spurring Israelis to flee from all of historic Palestine.

Over the past five years—and particularly since launching the satellite channel—al-Manar officials have repeatedly stated that they will begin broadcasting news and other programming in Hebrew in order to expand the station's sphere of influence among Israelis. Hebrew news bulletins were slated to begin in January 2001 but have been delayed for unspecified reasons. Any such broadcasts would reportedly involve members of the station's Hebrew Observation Department, which is charged with monitoring the Israeli press.

SUCCESS IN REACHING PRIMARY AUDIENCE

Although there are no official statistics regarding television ratings in the Middle East as a whole, al-Manar's own statistics show that its viewership has expanded dramatically over the years. This increase in popularity was particularly dramatic following Israel's withdrawal from southern Lebanon, which greatly heightened Hizballah's stature. Al-Manar's subscription to seven satellite providers led to a significant increase as well, expanding its viewership potential from the Levant to the entire globe.[63]

According to Nayef Krayem, the Israeli military, and other analysts, al-Manar ranks third in popularity among Lebanese viewers under normal conditions, but tops the rankings when events heat up in southern Lebanon or the Palestinian territories.[64] These and other sources also report that al-Manar and al-Jazeera are the two most popular stations in the West Bank and Gaza.[65] Al-Manar officials believe that their channel ranks among the top five most-watched throughout the Arab world, estimating that it draws approximately ten million viewers daily from around the world.[66] According to Mouafac Harb, vice president and director of network news for the Middle East Television Network (MTN), al-Manar is "gaining popularity in Lebanon, the Levant, North Africa, and even the GCC [Gulf Cooperation Council] countries."[67] This popularity helped the station win several awards at the eighth Cairo Television and Radio Festival in 2002. In fact, Hizballah's mass media outlets received the second most awards among a thousand competing television and radio programs.[68]

Additionally, in a March 2003 survey conducted in Jordan, participants were asked which television stations (both Western and Middle Eastern) they turned to first for news about "Palestine and the Palestinians." Al-Manar was the most popular choice with 28.8 percent of the responses, and al-Jazeera was second with 27.5 percent.[69]

Regardless of ratings data, the visceral effects of al-Manar's explicit programming should not be underestimated. In April 2002, for example, it was widely reported that Ayat al-Akhras, a female suicide bomber, had watched al-Manar incessantly before blowing herself up in front of a Jerusalem supermarket the previous month.[70]

BUDGET AND FUNDING

As of July 2002, al-Manar officials reported that the station was unprofitable and losing capital every year. "Annual financial losses are huge," Nayef Krayem maintained, but are covered by unnamed investors whose interests are "political rather than financial."[71] Moreover, although most television stations in the Arab world sell footage to other stations for profit, al-Manar prefers to swap its footage in return for what Krayem described as "favors or discounts" from other stations. These and other statements raise an important question: if al-Manar is, in fact, unprofitable, how has it been able to expand its viewership, procure a new high-tech building, purchase first-rate equipment from Sony, run four bureaus, and pay the salaries of reporters around the world? The answer, as indicated previously, is Iranian sponsorship.

At the time of al-Manar's founding, the station reportedly received seed money from Iran[72] and had a running budget of $1 million.[73] According to Krayem, its annual budget had grown to approximately $15 million by 2002.[74] Middle East analysts and journalists alike have reported that most of this funding comes from Iran.[75] Al-Manar officials vociferously deny this charge. Krayem maintained that the station receives no money from any government, claiming that al-Manar is in full compliance with Lebanese laws prohibiting stations from receiving foreign government funding.

This contention may be true from a purely technical standpoint. That is, Iran provides an estimated $100–200 million per year to Hizballah, which in turn transfers money to al-Manar, making Iranian funding of the station indirect.[76] Indeed, former al-Manar program director Sheikh Nasir al-Akhdar asserted that the station receives a large portion of its budget through "subsidies offered by the party [Hizballah]."[77] Al-Manar uses this symbiotic relationship as a legal loophole through which to skirt the law prohibiting foreign subsidies to Lebanese television stations.

Viewer support. Al-Manar's other major sources of income include donations from Shiite communities around the world and from other Arabs and Muslims who support Hizballah.[78] Numerous donations have reportedly been received from Muslim communities in Europe, the United States, and Canada.[79] During commercial breaks, al-Manar often requests that donors deposit money for Hizballah directly into accounts in four Lebanese banks (see video clips 11 and 12):

REFERENCE VIDEO CLIPS
11 and 12

- Beirut Riyadh Bank, Ghobeiri branch (account 46-01-465000-50156) and Mazraa branch (account 79131-3)
- Banque Libanaise pour le Commerce SAL, Ghobeiri branch, accounts 180146111266018000 and 401830
- Byblos Bank SAL, Haret Hreik branch, account 78-2-252-133521-1-5
- Fransa Bank, Cheiah branch, accounts 25010/69283021 and 78.02.251.133553.0.8

These deposits are requested in the name of funds such as the Association for Support of Islamic Resistance in Lebanon, the Intifada in Occupied Palestine fund, the Palestine Uprising fund, the Resistance Information Donation fund, and two other funds under Krayem's name. According to the clips mentioned above, the latter two funds serve as a "donation account for the resistance media [al-Manar Television]."

Corporate sponsors. Of secondary importance is the income that al-Manar receives from corporate sponsors. Since its founding in 1991, the station has had no shortage of commercial advertising from both Lebanese and Western companies. According to Ali Dahir, al-Manar's first general manager, the station has consistently turned down approximately 90 percent of potential clients because of questionable content, including the use of alcohol and "women as a temptation."[80]

Al-Manar has set up its own advertising company, Media-Publi Management, to manage its advertisers and promotion. This company has apparently worked with more than thirty-five advertising firms, including major international companies such as Saatchi and Saatchi.[81] As of 2004, commercial advertisements have been broadcast only on al-Manar's terrestrial outlet. This fact suggests that some companies may be trying to keep both their questionable advertising practices and their links to Hizballah away from the prying eyes of American viewers who have access to al-Manar's satellite channel. According to Krayem and other al-Manar officials, Pepsi, Coca-Cola, Procter and Gamble, and Western Union were among the station's largest American commercial advertisers as of July 2002.[82] Moreover, a random viewing of footage from al-Manar's terrestrial station in October 2002 uncovered several products advertised by other Western corporate sponsors, including Milka chocolate (German), Nestle's Nido milk (Swiss), Maggie Cubes (German), Smeds cheese and butter (Finnish), Picon cheese (French), Red Bull energy drink (Austrian), Gauloises cigarettes (French), and Henkel's Der General detergent (German). In late 2002, following a *Los Angeles Times* op-ed by the author, the above-named U.S. companies ceased advertising on al-Manar; the European companies continued, however.[83] On December 10 of that year, twenty-two members of Congress sent a letter urging the Bush administration to prohibit U.S. companies from advertising on al-Manar.[84]

Other sources. Al-Manar also reportedly receives small amounts of funding from Hizballah business ventures and cooperatives in Beirut, southern Lebanon, and the Bekaa Valley.[85] Hizballah's role in these ventures—which reportedly include construction companies, heavy machinery manufacturers, and drug trafficking operations—has not been publicly disclosed. Al-Manar also receives income from "renting out some of its operational equipment to Arab or foreign stations covering events in Lebanon."[86]

INVOLVEMENT IN TERRORISM

Al-Manar has been deeply involved in Palestinian terrorist activity against Israel, and the station views such support as a badge of honor. Indeed, al-Manar has presented itself as a war room for Palestinian terrorism, to be used for reporting events, claiming responsibility for attacks, and discussing terror strategy. Nasrallah highlighted the station's support for the Palestinian cause in a November 2000 interview on Syrian television:

> The victory in southern Lebanon is dedicated to the Palestinian nation. Through al-Manar, we are offering moral and communication support dedicated entirely to the Palestinian issue. Hizballah understands how important television is to the resistance in Lebanon as it is for the intifada, and so there are broadcasts on al-Manar from the morning till midnight, all of them on the Palestinian issue.[87]

When asked to specify what sort of operational assistance Hizballah gives to the Palestinians, Hizballah officials generally demur or answer "propaganda assistance." For example, on December 31, 2000, Hizballah deputy secretary-general Sheikh Naim Qassam told Lebanese Future Television that Hizballah provides "national support to the Palestinians through al-Manar television," but he was unwilling to discuss actual military or monetary aid.[88] In June 2002, however, Sheikh Hassan Izz al-Din, a member of Hizballah's Political Council and the party's director for media relations, declared, "We support the Palestinian cause politically, financially, ethically, and morally. We provide [the Palestinians] with weapons, training, and whatever they need. We are there to stand by their side." As one Lebanese journalist stated during an appearance on al-Manar,

> It is no secret that Hizballah assists in the intifada. Hizballah does not need to write reports about its support for the Palestinians. It is not a secret—we all know that Hizballah provides direct aid and support to the intifada and the resistance not only through the mass media.[89]

Al-Manar itself is clearly linked to Palestinian violence through its calls for resistance and its ties to terrorist organizations. Nayef Krayem admitted that the station had close contacts with "all Palestinian groups" through emails, phone calls, and faxes. According to him, Palestinians "do whatever is necessary to send us material." Indeed, from the beginning of the intifada, al-Manar has served as the preferred outlet for Palestinian rejectionist groups claiming responsibility for attacks against Israelis. Groups that have made such claims on the station include the following: the Forces of Umar al-Mukhtar (Quwat Umar al-Mukhtar, a code name for the military wing of Fatah's Abu Musa faction);[90] the al-Aqsa Martyrs Brigades (Kitaib Shuhada al-Aqsa);[91] the Jerusalem Brigades (Kitaib al-Quds, the military wing of PIJ);[92] the Badr Brigades (Quwat Badr);[93] the Brigades of Return (Kitaib al-Awda, a code name for Hamas); the Izz al-Din al-Qassam Brigades (Kitaib Izz al-Din al-Qassam, the military wing of Hamas); the Salah al-Din Brigades (Kitaib Salah al-Din, one of the names used when groups such as Hamas, Fatah, and others engage in cooperative operations);[94] and the Black Oslo Brigades (Kitaib Oslo al-Aswad, a name of convenience for an unknown group). Al-Manar has also featured spokesmen from terrorist organizations providing details of various attacks.

Moreover, in promoting violent, zero-sum "solutions" to the Israeli-Palestinian conflict, al-Manar programming frequently praises suicide bombing (see "Legitimizing Suicide Operations" in chapter 4). Indeed, station officials maintain that one of al-Manar's aims is to promote suicide missions. The station also strives to ensure that the families of suicide bombers know that they will be compensated for their loss (see video clip 13).

REFERENCE VIDEO CLIP
13

In addition, al-Manar sometimes possesses exclusive information regarding a host of Palestinian activities. For example, in a news bulletin from January 28, 2001, the station reported that boxes of ammunition, including rocket-propelled grenade launchers, had been "floated" (that is, thrown off a ship and carried to shore by the tide) to Gaza and picked up by the Palestinian security services. This incident was not reported by any other television outlet until several days later; even then, Palestinian Authority officials vehemently denied the story. The smuggling episode was not widely reported or confirmed until many weeks after al-Manar had announced it, demonstrating the station's superior access to officials in the Palestinian territories.

Moreover, a number of al-Manar's own reporters are involved with Palestinian terrorist and rejectionist groups. For example, Imad I'id, the station's permanent reporter in Gaza, is linked to PIJ, having written for that organization's newspaper, *al-Istiqlal*. Dib Hourani, who served as al-Manar's reporter in Jenin, is also close to sources in Fatah.[95] Issa Zawahara, an al-Manar reporter in the Palestinian territories, has been linked to PIJ and has served time in Israeli and Palestinian jails.[96] Fuad Hussein, al-Manar's correspondent in Amman, identifies himself as an Islamist activist in the Jordanian Committee against Normalization with Israel.[97]

Al-Manar employees have been linked to terrorist activity in other parts of the world as well. In June 2002, as part of a federal court ruling in Charlotte, North Carolina, two Hizballah operatives—brothers Muhammad and Chawki Hammoud—were convicted of providing material support to a terrorist group. The cell had two branches: one based in the United States and the other in Canada. The Charlotte-based branch was responsible for raising funds and procuring dual-use technologies for Hizballah. The Canadian branch purchased night-vision goggles, global positioning systems, stun guns, naval equipment, nitrogen cutters, and laser range finders in Canada and the United States and then smuggled them into Lebanon.[98]

During the course of the federal trial, it was revealed that Muhammad Dbouk, one of the leaders of the Canadian cell, had engaged in preoperational surveillance on behalf of Hizballah while using his al-Manar journalist credentials. Dbouk had filmed Israeli military targets in southern Lebanon, and the footage was subsequently used by Hizballah militants to plan suicide bombings and other attacks on those targets. In addition, Dbouk accompanied Hizballah's guerrilla units on their attack missions, filmed the live attacks, and used the footage to produce propaganda videos for the organization. According to Matthew Levitt, the U.S. government's expert witness in the Hammoud case, Dbouk's videos "were found in the homes of the Charlotte cell members, where they were used to solicit funds at local gatherings."[99] Cases such as this completely debunk the myth that Hizballah's militant activities can be divorced from its so-called "political wing."

TARGETED PROGRAMMING

Al-Manar's primetime programming is made up of a variety of elements. Approximately 25 percent is devoted to music videos and other filler, 25 percent to talk shows, 25 percent to series and dramas, and the remaining 25 percent to news and family shows (see appendix for a detailed outline). Throughout the 1990s, al-Manar was Lebanon's leading producer of in-house programming. By 1994, the station was producing 50 percent of its own material, and by 2003, the figure approached 70 percent. This increase reflects Hizballah's preference for self-produced programming and a desire to preserve "the integrity of Islamic and cultural programming."[100]

As discussed in chapter 2, up until 2000, the station tended to air programs focusing on events inside Lebanon. Early programming included a cornucopia of serial shows, movies, news programs, children's shows, and regular news bulletins.[101] In the early 1990s, programming began at 4:15 p.m. with readings from the Quran followed by children's shows and cartoons. The station also focused on religious figures and clerics associated with Hizballah in a program titled *Khitab al-Qaid*, or *In the Words of the Commander*. For example, Ayatollah Ruhollah Khomeini and Sheikh Abbas Musawi, Hizballah's second secretary-general, made frequent appearances.

While featuring programs that heavily emphasized religion and prayer, the station also aired series and movies from Iran, the Arab world, and even the United States (all censored for

Avi Jorisch

violence and sexual content, according to Muhammad Afif Ahmed, the station's second general manager).[102] Docudramas and programs dedicated to guerrillas who died fighting against Israel also aired regularly. Other broadcasts included foreign documentaries, sports events, political talk shows, and propaganda and music videos aired during commercial breaks. The music videos, which initially focused on the Israeli occupation of Lebanon, featured footage filmed by crews accompanying guerrillas in southern Lebanon.

As described previously, between May and September 2000—the period following Israel's withdrawal from Lebanon and leading up to the outbreak of the Palestinian intifada—the tone of al-Manar programming changed significantly. More propaganda videos were shown, highlighting Israel's withdrawal, Hizballah's military campaign, the south's liberation, and Israel's supposed military weakness. Music videos began to emphasize the themes of "triumph over Israel" and "liberation of southern Lebanon." In pandering to its Lebanese constituents (especially those residing in southern Lebanon), Hizballah was attempting to garner support for the September 2000 Lebanese parliamentary elections.

With the outbreak of the intifada, both al-Manar and Hizballah's focus acutely shifted from the Lebanese to the Israeli-Palestinian arena. Along with Hizballah's other mass media branches (i.e., al-Nur radio, *al-Intiqad* newspaper, and several websites), al-Manar soon publicly offered its services to the Palestinians. The station focused heavily on inciting Palestinians to violence, encouraging them to refuse negotiations for a comprehensive settlement with Israel and to work toward the obliteration of the Jewish state.

In another move suggesting solidarity with the intifada, al-Manar began to list its program times according to "Occupied Jerusalem Time" instead of Beirut Standard Time (the two time zones are identical). In addition, the station expanded its news bulletins to concentrate on the intifada. This coverage came at the expense of internal Lebanese coverage, which was relegated to the end portion of news bulletins. The new coverage included interviews with leaders of Palestinian rejectionist and terrorist organizations, including Ramadan Abdallah Shallah (secretary-general of PIJ) (see video clip 14), Marwan Barghouti (leader of the Fatah Tanzim militias), Khalid Mishal (head of the political bureau of Hamas), Mousa Abu Marzouk (Hamas spokesman), and Abdel Aziz Rantisi (one of Hamas's chief spokesmen to foreign media). Al-Manar also produced and aired a documentary series reenacting Israel's assassination of PIJ founder Fathi Shiqaqi. In contrast, the station aired very few interviews with Palestinian

REFERENCE VIDEO CLIP

14

Authority officials, who were shunned for negotiating with Israel and regarded as apologists for the Jewish state.

As the intifada wore on, al-Manar typically reported Israeli military operations and Palestinian attacks in the form of special news flashes. Moreover, many of the station's programs included guests who were asked to express their often vitriolic opinions on the situation in the Palestinian territories. Viewers were encouraged to call in from around the Arab world to voice support for the intifada. Many viewers, especially Palestinians, took this opportunity to thank Hizballah for the aid it was providing.

Meanwhile, al-Manar's music videos soon began to combine footage of Hizballah attacks on Israeli military installations and footage of Palestinian clashes with the IDF. Juxtaposing such images sent a clear message that the two struggles should be regarded as one, and that the lessons of Hizballah's successes in Lebanon should be applied to the Palestinian uprising. According to

REFERENCE VIDEO CLIP
15

this reasoning, Hizballah's model of liberating southern Lebanon could serve as a model for liberating 1948 Palestine (i.e., the West Bank, Gaza, and all of the territory constituting Israel). Al-Manar continues to disseminate this view, airing videos that offer brief accounts of past Hizballah and Palestinian operations against Israel (see video clip 15).

Other propaganda videos aired in the wake of the intifada sought to depict Israel as weak by "exposing" both its fear of suicide bombers and its military defeat in Lebanon. Such programming was aimed at shattering the myth of the "invincible IDF" and promoting the "Lebanonization" of the Israeli-Palestinian conflict. Hizballah reasoned that if Palestinians adopted its model, Israelis would be unable to handle the pressure, and the fabric of Israeli society would unravel.

Al-Manar's propaganda videos also began to call for Arab unity in dismantling the Zionist entity. In this context, the station repeatedly emphasized Jerusalem. Videos depicted Hizballah guerrillas marching in the direction of Jerusalem, accompanied by footage of riots on the Temple Mount and of Hizballah operations against the IDF in southern Lebanon. The implication was that Hizballah fighters would eventually march south to liberate Jerusalem.

During this period, al-Manar also altered its programming to target Israeli Arabs. Propaganda videos called on Arab citizens of Israel to join the Palestinian struggle, with some comparing Israel to Nazi Germany by transforming the Star of David into a swastika. Indeed, when the intifada first erupted, riots broke out in several Israeli Arab towns. Community leaders incited citizens to violate laws, commit violence against Israeli police, and remove flags and other symbols of Israeli sovereignty. Cries of "death to the Jews" and "we will redeem Palestine with blood and fire" were heard among the masses of rioters.[103] Thirteen Israeli Arabs were killed in clashes with Israeli police, further inflaming tensions and giving Hizballah's message even greater resonance.

Al-Manar also took pains to emphasize the memory of *shuhada,* or holy martyrs, who died in the service of either the intifada or Hizballah. For example, the station repeatedly showed footage of Muhammad al-Dura, a twelve-year-old boy who was shot and killed during a clash between the IDF and Palestinian gunmen.[104] Such images were meant to focus the attention of the Arab world on the vicious cycle of violence and to drum up anger toward Israel for "killing its children."

Al-Manar sought to provoke further anti-Israeli—and anti-American—sentiment through its coverage of the al-Qaeda terrorist attacks of September 11, 2001. Many in the Arab world still accept as fact the notion that "Jews, Israel, and the Mossad" perpetrated those attacks. Such allegations have appeared on numerous websites and chat rooms, as well as in newspapers and news broadcasts throughout the Middle East.[105] The first known mention of Israeli involvement in the attacks occurred in a September 17, 2001, report by none other than al-Manar. In addition, Hizballah posted the allegation on its website on September 18, 2001.[106] The *Washington Post* confirmed that the story "originated with a September 17 report by the Beirut-based Manar television network."[107] The newspaper quoted an al-Manar official who stated, "If we did not believe it, then we would not have published it."

Specifically, al-Manar's allegations—which the station falsely attributed to the Jordanian newspaper *al-Watan*—claimed that "4,000 Israelis remained absent" from the World Trade Center on September 11 "based on hints from the Israeli general security apparatus, the Shabak."[108] Only al-Manar claims to have actually seen this editorial in *al-Watan,* and the article is not available in the tiny Jordanian newspaper's online archives. In a December 2001 interview in the Spanish daily *El Mundo,* Hassan Nasrallah stated that al-Manar

> didn't make that story up....It just limited itself to reproducing what was being said, even if we're not totally sure that the theory is true. The point is, you have to look at all the hypotheses, because you can't rule out any option just yet and neither can you clearly point to one movement as being responsible for what happened."[109]

REFERENCE VIDEO CLIP
16

In any case, the station continued to disseminate conspiracy theories about the attacks well after the fact (see video clip 16).

More recently, the war in Iraq gave al-Manar an opportunity to train its sights on yet another target. As mentioned previously, from the outset of Operation Iraqi Freedom, the station demonstrated its strongly anti-American mindset through its coverage of the hostilities. Specifically, al-Manar began to direct a significant amount of its existing programming (e.g., talk shows, music videos, news bulletins) and propaganda tactics toward the goal of inciting violence against U.S. forces (see chapter 3).

JOURNALISTIC INTEGRITY?

Al-Manar officials claim that the station refrains from needless diatribes in its programming and strives to strike a balanced tone in its reporting.[110] As one official put it, "We broadcast what Hamas says, what Arafat says, what the Israelis say, what America says. Our reporting is objective."[111] A review of al-Manar programming clearly demonstrates the opposite. The lan-

REFERENCE VIDEO CLIP
17

guage that the station uses is certainly not objective. For example, al-Manar presents suicide bombings as a laudable phenomenon by labeling them *amaliyat istishahidiya* (martyrdom operations). Similarly, pictures of suicide bombers are often flashed across the screen during commercial breaks, paying tribute to their memory and showing respect for their actions (see video clip 17). The same pictures are prominently displayed at al-Manar's Beirut office.

Moreover, the station's reporters usually refer to Israeli officials as "Ministers of the enemy Israel." Former al-Manar editor-in-chief Hussein Rahal stated, "As for [Yitzhak] Rabin or [Shimon] Peres, the presenter obviously will say 'the prime minister or the foreign minister of the enemy.'"[112] As a rule, the word "Israel" is avoided. Instead, the country is referred to as the "Zionist entity," the "Zionist enemy," or "Palestine '48," while Jewish communities in the Galilee are called "settlements in northern Palestine."[113]

By refusing to call Israel by its name, by explicitly calling for acts of violence such as suicide bombings, by involving its reporters in militant attacks, and through various other activities, al-Manar has clearly exhibited characteristics inconsistent with professional and objective reporting. Although some of its programming resembles that of a credible news channel, al-Manar presents deeply biased views and blatantly disseminates propaganda.

NOTES

1. Information obtained from an Israeli military document dated October 22, 2002.

2. Magda Abu Fadil, "Hezbollah TV Takes Credit for Ousting Israelis," *IPI Global Journalist 6,* no. 4 (fourth quarter, 2000). Available online (www.freemedia.at/IPIReport4.00/ipirep4.00_3.htm).

3. Ali Dahir, interview, al-Nahar (Beirut), September 2, 1992.

4. John Lancaster, "Hezbollah Tunes In on Profits; Party's TV Station Airing U.S. Movies," *Washington Post,* June 19, 1995.

5. Interview with Middle East media expert granted to author on condition of anonymity, Washington, D.C., December 17, 2002. See also Nicholas Blanford, "Hizballah Gives al-Manar TV More Authority in Media Wing Reshuffle," *Daily Star* (Beirut), August 4, 2001.

6. Al-Manar's board of directors has nine members and forty shareholders, most of whom are members of Hizballah.

7. Unless otherwise indicated, all quotes attributed to al-Manar and Hizballah personnel were obtained from the individuals in question during interviews conducted at the Beirut station on June 27–28, 2002. The titles attributed to these personnel represent the positions they held at the time of the interviews.

8. The men died on consecutive days in July 1993. See Robert Fisk, "Television News Is Secret Weapon of the Intifada," *The Independent* (London), December 2, 2000. See also Jacques Lhuillery, "Hezbollah TV: Waging a Broadcasting War against Israel," Agence France Presse, February 5, 1995, and Hugh Dellios, "With an Eye towards Politics, Hezbollah Recasting Its Image; Savvy TV Campaign Credited in Group's Battle with Israel," *Chicago Tribune,* April 13, 2000.

9. Al-Manar also intends to build studios at the basement level, an idea modeled on al-Jazeera's studios in Qatar, which al-Manar reporters visited in 2001. Both the United States and Israel have demonstrated that they regard "hostile" media organizations as legitimate military targets. Examples include Israeli operations against Hizballah's al-Fajr radio station in 1994 and the U.S. strikes against Radio/Television Serbia in Belgrade in 1999 and against al-Jazeera's Kabul headquarters in 2001.

10. Charles Radin, "Hezbollah Gains Clout as Political, Social Force," *Boston Globe,* August 19, 2001.

11. Lhuillery, "Hezbollah TV: Waging a Broadcasting War."

12. Fisk, "Television News Is Secret Weapon." See also Bassem Mroue, "TV Station of Lebanon's Hezbollah Guerrillas Shows Historical Drama with Relevance to Today's Palestinian Uprising," Associated Press, November 28, 2001.

13. "Hezbollah to Set Up Hebrew TV Station, Web Site," *al-Istiqlal,* November 18, 1999, BBC Summary of World Broadcasts, December 3, 1999. *Al-Istiqlal* is a Gaza-based newspaper published by Palestinian Islamic Jihad. The precise meaning of the phrase "occupied territories" in this quote is unclear. It could indicate Palestinians from either Israel or the West Bank and Gaza.

14. Magda Abu Fadil, "Al-Manar TV: No Love for U.S. but No Help from Taliban," Poynter Online, October 23, 2001. Available online (www.poynter.org/content/content_view.asp?id=16466). See also Fisk, "Television News Is Secret Weapon," p. 16. In that December 2000 article, Nayef Krayem stated, "We already have a programme about the Israeli media presented by an ex-prisoner called Adel Termos who translates from Hebrew. He does live translations from Hebrew into Arabic when [then–Israeli prime minister] Ehud Barak gives a press conference." In addition, al-Manar's Hebrew

Observation Department monitors Israeli media broadcasts and the Hebrew press. When suicide bombings occur, al-Manar often pirates footage from both Israeli Broadcasting Authority Channel 1 and commercial television Channel 2 and subsequently beams it to viewers in real time. When asked about pirating Israeli television programming, Krayem asserted, "[The Israelis] steal footage from us, and we steal footage from them. There is a mutual unspoken agreement that we can steal from them and [they] from us." In a particularly revealing comment, he added, "This is the only peaceful exchange that we have with the Israelis." For an interesting article covering this topic, see Jacki Hugi, "The Voice of Quiet Thunder," *Maariv Sofshavua* supplement (in Hebrew), July 26, 2002.

15. See Lhuillery, "Hezbollah TV: Waging a Broadcasting War."

16. "Independent and Leftist, Espousing Arab Nationalist Views," *al-Safir* (Beirut), March 3, 1997.

17. Abu Fadil, "Hezbollah TV Takes Credit."

18. The Jordanian bureau was opened before the first anniversary of Israel's redeployment from Lebanon. Jordanian information minister Talib al-Rifaʻi made the initial commitment to open the bureau in April 2001. See "Jordan to Grant Hezbollah TV Licence to Open Office in Amman by 25 May," al-Manar Television, May 1, 2001, BBC Worldwide Monitoring, May 31, 2000. See also Ibrahim Khayat, "Hamas Prepares to Start a Television Station and al-Manar Opens an Office in Amman" (in Arabic), *al-Hayat* (Beirut), April 30, 2001. Rifaʻi also stated that "regimes sooner or later will realise that they cannot prevent the flow of information and that with the globalisation of technology has come the globalisation of information." See Eman Abdullah, "Greater Openness by Official Media: A Big Step to Democracy," *Gulf News,* April 30, 2001, in Financial Times Information, Global News Wire, April 30, 2001. When asked why al-Manar needed an office in Jordan, Krayem maintained, "We had certain production needs that we felt could be better done with an office in Jordan." The current manager of al-Manar's Amman office is Fuad Hussein.

19. These correspondents change locations regularly. As of June 2003, al-Manar reporters were stationed in Amman (Fuad Hussein), Baghdad (Ahmed al-Askari and Diyan al-Nasiri), Brussels (Kamal Badr), Cairo (Mahmud al-Bakri), Jordan (Dib al-Karala), Kuwait (Suleiman al-Asusi), Paris (Wlis Shrara), Turkey (Hasan al-Taharawi), and Washington (Muhammad Dalbah).

20. "Hezbollah TV Broadcasts Live Clashes with Israelis," al-Manar, April 8, 2002, BBC Summary of World Broadcasts, April 8, 2002. See also Nicholas Blanford, "Hezbullah Sharpens Its Weapons in Propaganda War," *Christian Science Monitor,* December 28, 2001.

21. Abu Fadil, "Al-Manar TV: No Love."

22. Dellios, "With an Eye towards Politics." See also "Hezbollah Inaugurates Satellite Channel via ArabSat," al-Raʻy (Amman), May 29, 2000, BBC Summary of World Broadcasts, May 31, 2000.

23. Abu Fadil, "Al-Manar TV: No Love."

24. The first noncommercial television station in the Arab world was established by the Iraqi government in Baghdad in 1957. See Nabil Dajani, "The Changing Scene of Lebanese Television," *Transnational Broadcasting Studies,* no. 7 (Fall–Winter 2001). Available online (www.tbsjournal.com/Archives/Fall01/dajani.html).

25. Clause J of the accord calls for the following: "To reorganize all media under the law and within the framework of responsible freedom, and in a manner that serves the objectives of reconciliation and of ending the state of war." See Habib Malik, *Between Damascus and Jerusalem: Lebanon and Middle East Peace* (Washington, D.C.: The Washington Institute for Near East Policy, 2000), p. 121.

26. Martin Regg Cohn, "Lebanon's War of the Airwaves: TV Pirates Balk at Clampdown on Stations Run without a License," *Toronto Star*, May 18, 1996. Under the same law, the government licensed only eleven radio stations. See "Lebanese Officials Accused of 'Dividing the Spoils' in Licensing Media," Mideast Mirror, September 19, 1996.

27. According to Habib Malik, Lebanon is home to eighteen different religious denominations. See Malik, *Between Damascus and Jerusalem*.

28. The shareholders of LBCI included prominent members of the government. During the civil war, the Christian Lebanese Forces ran the station. See "Hezbollah Stages Political Comeback As Curtain Falls on Lebanese Elections," Mideast Mirror, September 17, 1996.

29. "Private Media Employees Protest Law to Scrap Illegal TVs, Radios," Agence France Presse, January 23, 1996. Approximately fifty unlicensed private television stations and 150 radio stations were operating in Lebanon before the new laws were passed. As mentioned previously, most of those stations emerged during the civil war and were controlled by the various militias. See "Private Media Employees Protest Law to Scrap Illegal TVs, Radios," Agence France Presse, January 23, 1996. See also "Further on Licensing of Television, Radio Stations," Middle East News Agency, September 17, 1996; "Press Watchdog Protests New Broadcast Regulations in Lebanon," Agence France Presse, February 9, 1996; "Lebanon Licenses 15 Radio and TV Stations," Radio Lebanon, September 17, 1996, BBC Summary of World Broadcasts, September 20, 1996; and Cohn, "Lebanon's War of the Airwaves."

30. Nayef Krayem, interview by author, al-Manar Television station, Beirut, June 27, 2002. See also "Lebanese Officials Accused of 'Dividing the Spoils.'" A total of sixty-three television and radio stations applied for licenses but only sixteen received them. See also "Hezbollah Stages Political Comeback," and Sam Ghattas, "Government Restricts TV, Radio Broadcasts," Associated Press, September 17, 1996.

31. "Hezbollah Pleased with Decision to License Television," Deutsche Presse-Agentur, July 28, 1997. After al-Manar secured its license, a Hizballah official was quoted in the Lebanese press as saying, "They licensed us because we are the voice of the resistance against Israel....Our strugglers are redeeming their blood for the sake of liberating the land." The other three stations received their licenses in 1999. New TV, run by Tahsin Hayat, an outspoken opponent of Prime Minister Hariri, remains fully operational today ("Lebanon Grants License to TV Station after Three-Year Closure," Deutsche Presse-Agentur, June 24, 1999). The Independent Communication Channel International (ICNI) and United Television (UTV), although no longer operating full time, nevertheless broadcast a minimal amount in order to keep their licenses (Dajani, "The Changing Scene of Lebanese Television"). A fourth station—the Christian religious outlet called Tele-Lumiere—"continues to broadcast without a license, but with tacit government approval" (Ibid.).

32. Interview with Middle East media expert granted to author on condition of anonymity, Washington, D.C., December 17, 2002. See also Nicholas Blanford, "Hizballah Gives al-Manar TV More Authority in Media Wing Reshuffle," *Daily Star* (Beirut), August 4, 2001.

33. Dajani, "The Changing Scene of Lebanese Television."

34. LBCI is uplinked from Rome and announces contact addresses in Lebanon and Dubai. See "Clandestine and Other Selected Broadcasts," BBC Summary of World Broadcasts, September 7, 1998.

35. Reuven Paz, "Hizballah Considering Satellite Broadcasts," International Policy Institute for Counter-Terrorism (ICT), March 22, 2000. See also "Lebanon's Hezbollah Claims Its Share of the Satellite TV Market," *al-Hayat* (London), March 9, 2000, Mideast Mirror, March 9, 2000.

36. "Lebanon: Cabinet Approves al-Manar Satellite Transmission," *al-Safir* website, April 6, 2000, BBC Worldwide Monitoring, April 7, 2000.

37. See also "Hezbollah Inaugurates Satellite Channel via ArabSat."

38. Hale Cabbabe (assistant to executive manager, Murr Television), interview by author, Murr Television station, Beirut, July 2, 2002.

39. Tahsin Hayat (chairman of the board of directors and owner, New TV), interview by author, New TV headquarters, Beirut, June 26, 2002.

40. Bassam Mroue, "Authorities Close Down Anti-Syrian Christian Television Station," Associated Press, September 4, 2002.

41. "Lebanese Murr Television Appeals Court Order to Close Down," Associated Press, October 28, 2002.

42. The station has a secondary website as well (www.dm.net.lb/almanar).

43. See also "Hezbollah Inaugurates Satellite Channel via ArabSat."

44. Ali Dahir, interview, *al-Nahar* (Beirut), September 2, 1992.

45. "Hezbollah's Voice of Light Radio Station Not Licensed," *al-Nahar* (Beirut), July 25, 1997, BBC Summary of World Broadcasts, August 1, 1997. See also "Hezbollah Inaugurates Satellite Channel via ArabSat."

46. "Al-Manar Television to Start Test Broadcasting Shortly," *al-Diyar* (Beirut), May 27, 1991.

47. Ali Dahir, interview.

48. Ibid.

49. Information obtained from an Israeli military document dated October 22, 2002.

50. "Hezbollah Inaugurates Satellite Channel via ArabSat." See also "Lebanon's Hezbollah Claims Its Share."

51. Frank Sesno and Brent Sadler, "Crisis in the Middle East: Al-Manar Airs Hezbollah's High-Tech Propaganda Campaign," *CNN Newsday*, October 26, 2000.

52. Ibid.

53. Bill Samii, "Washington Asks Tehran to Restrain Hezbollah," Radio Free Europe, April 16, 2002, Financial Times Information, Global News Wire, April 16, 2002.

54. "Hizballah's al-Manar Carries Palestinian Television's Logo in Broadcasts," *al-Sharq al-Awsat* (London), December 14, 2001, BBC Summary of World Broadcasts, December 14, 2001.

55. Ibid. This "solidarity" should not be confused with support for the Palestinian Authority (PA). Al-Manar officials have repeatedly refused to link Hizballah's political position with Yasser Arafat. According to them, the station's decision to display the Palestinian Television logo was more "in line with its hostility toward Israel" than any identification with the PA.

56. Abu Fadil, "Al-Manar TV: No Love." See also Blanford, "Hezbullah Sharpens Its Weapons."

57. "Hezbollah to Set Up Hebrew TV Station, Web Site."

58. Abu Fadil, "Al-Manar TV: No Love."

59. "Hezbollah to Set Up Hebrew TV Station, Web Site."

60. "Hezbollah's Media Outlets Detailed," al-Manar Television (Beirut), September 11, 1998, BBC Summary of World Broadcasts, September 23, 1998.

61. Paz, "Hizballah Considering Satellite Broadcasts."

62. Many Israeli Arabs, along with Palestinians residing in the West Bank and Gaza, receive al-Manar directly because they own satellite dishes that carry ArabSat.

63. As of August 2004, Al-Manar broadcast its programming on the following seven packages: IntelSat, broadcasting to North America; New Skies Satellites (NSS) 803, broadcasting to Africa and parts of Europe; ArabSat 3a, broadcasting to the Middle East, North Africa, and parts of Europe; NileSat 101, broadcasting to the Middle East, North Africa, and parts of Europe; HispaSat, broadcasting to South America; AsiaSat 35, broadcasting to Asia; and EutelSat, broadcasting to Europe and parts of North Africa. From al-Manar's Beirut studios, the signal is sent to two distributors—Globecast and ArabSat (as noted above, ArabSat also acts as a direct provider)—and directly to NileSat. ArabSat in turn sells its Arabic package (which includes al-Manar) to HispaSat, AsiaSat, EutelSat, and New Skies Satellites. Globecast sells its Arabic package to the American provider IntelSat. See "Marketing Terror: How Hizballah Spreads Propaganda and Hate around the World through al-Manar" (in Hebrew), Intelligence and Terrorism Information Center at the Center for Special Studies, September 19, 2004 (available online at www.intelligence.org.il/sp/9_04/almanar.htm); additional information regarding al-Manar's satellite packages can be found on the website LyngSat Address (see www.sat-address.com/ab/Al-Manar-TV.html).

    Further rounding out the picture is a study conducted by Radwan al-Hamrouni and Adel al-Sahbani, which presents a slightly different account. According to them, al-Manar's satellite signal is broadcast from the Beirut control room to two digital uplinks at ArabSat 3a and NileSat 101. Arabsat then sells the package to Globecast in Berceneaye, France. From there, the signal is sent through cables to Serte, France, where it is transformed into NTSC color format. The signal is then sent under the Atlantic Ocean to Culver, California, via fiber-optic cables. Finally, the signal is sent to the Intelsat/Telstar 5 satellite package, from which it can then be viewed through-out Canada and northern Mexico without a monthly fee. From Berceneaye, the signal is also sent to NSS 803 (after which it can be viewed throughout Africa). See Radwan al-Hamrouni and Adel al-Sahbani, "War Media and Resistance Media: Al-Manar Television As Case Study," master's the-sis, Institute of the Press and News Sciences, Tunisian Ministry of Higher Education, 2001–2002.

64. See John Daniszewski, "Onetime Fanatical Menace Now Savior to Many Lebanese," *Los Angeles Times,* May 11, 2000. Additional information obtained from an Israeli military document dated October 22, 2002. See also "Hizballah TV Gaining Popularity," *Jerusalem Post,* June 14, 2004 (available online at www.jpost.com/servlet/Satellite?pagename=JPost/JPArticle/Printer&cid=1087182009525&p=1078113566627); Blanford, "Hezbullah Sharpens Its Weapons"; and Karim Alrawi, "Media in the New Iraq," *Arab Reform Bulletin* 2, no. 1 (January 2004) (available online at www.carnegieendowment.org/publications/index.cfm?fa=view&id=1446#Media).

65. Ibid. See also James Kitfield, "The Hezbollah Model," *National Journal,* May 18, 2002.

66. See Christopher Dickey, "The Iran Connection," *Newsweek,* February 18, 2002, and Neil MacFarquhar, "Hezbollah Becomes Potent Anti-U.S. Force," *New York Times,* December 24, 2002.

67. Mouafac Harb, telephone interview by author, November 6, 2003.

68. Al-Manar received four awards (two gold and two silver), and Hizballah's al-Nur radio station earned nine awards (six gold and three silver). "Lebanon Brief News: Hizbullah's Broadcasting Arms Garner Awards," Lebanonwire, July 12, 2002. Available online (www.lebanonwire.com/0207/02071201DS.asp).

69. Shibley Telhami, "Arab Country Media Survey," poll conducted in Jordan in cooperation with Zogby International, March 12, 2003.

70. Joshua Hammer, "How Two Lives Met in Death," *Newsweek,* April 15, 2002.

71. See also Radin, "Hezbollah Gains Clout," and Blanford, "Hezbullah Sharpens Its Weapons."

72. Interview with Lebanese Hizballah expert granted to author on condition of anonymity, October 11, 2002.

73. Blanford, "Hezbullah Sharpens Its Weapons."

74. See also Abu Fadil, "Hezbollah TV Takes Credit." Former al-Manar director of programming Sheikh Nasir al-Akhdar stated that al-Manar's budget is less than one-fourth that of other Lebanese satellite channels ("Hezbollah Inaugurates Satellite Channel via ArabSat"). According to Krayem, the station spends approximately 25 percent of this budget to broadcast on its first six satellite dish packages. Al-Manar's $15 million budget is nearly half the size of al-Jazeera's annual budget (Muhammad Jasem al-Ali, interview by author, al-Jazeera television station, Qatar, June 18, 2002; at the time of the interview, al-Ali was a board member and managing editor at al-Jazeera).

75. For example, Robert Fisk, one of England's premier journalists, "suspects that Iran provides much of the cash" for al-Manar (Fisk, "Television News Is Secret Weapon"). When station officials are asked directly about their sources of funding, they often answer by raising their hands toward heaven and "invoking the generosity of God."

76. Ali Nuri Zada, "Iran Raises Budget of 'Islamic Jihad' and Appropriates Funds to Previous Fighters," *al-Sharq al-Awsat* (London), June 8, 2000. English translation of article available online (www.cia.gov/cia/public_affairs/speeches/archives/1996/dci_speech_022296.html). See also Gal Luft, "Hizballahland," *Commentary,* July–August 2003; Gary Ackerman and Laura Snyder, "Would They If They Could?" *Bulletin of Atomic Scientists* 58, no. 3 (May 1, 2002), p. 41; Boaz Ganor, "Countering State-Sponsored Terrorism," International Policy Institute for Counter-Terrorism, p. 4 (available online at www.ict.org.il/articles/articledet.cfm?articleid=5#Conflicts); and Amit Cohen, "Shuvo Shel Ha-iyum Hatzfoni" (The return of the northern threat), *Maariv* (Tel Aviv), December 6, 2002.

77. "Hezbollah Inaugurates Satellite Channel via ArabSat." Similarly, some analysts maintain that the station depends on "monthly assistance from Hizballah." Hamrouni and Sahbani, "War Media and Resistance Media."

78. Charlotte Edwardes, "Hezbollah's Islamic Revolution Goes Online: Terrorist Group Takes Lesson from West to Promote Its Cause," *Calgary Herald,* September 11, 1999.

79. "Hezbollah Inaugurates Satellite Channel via ArabSat."

80. Ali Dahir, interview, *al-Nahar* (Beirut), September 2, 1992.

81. Lhuillery, "Hezbollah TV: Waging a Broadcasting War."

82. See also Maher Chmaytelli, "Hezbollah Wages War on the Small Screen," Agence France Presse, April 17, 1996 (this article named both Coca-Cola and Pepsi as al-Manar advertisers). See also Lhuillery, "Hezbollah TV: Waging a Broadcasting War."

83. Avi Jorisch, "Hezbollah Hate with a U.S. Link," *Los Angeles Times,* October 13, 2002.

84. Press release from Representative Henry Waxman (D-Calif.), December 10, 2002.

85. Edwardes, "Hezbollah's Islamic Revolution Goes Online."

86. Hamrouni and Sahbani, "War Media and Resistance Media."

87. Quote obtained from an Israeli military document dated October 22, 2002.

88. Ibid.

89. Ibrahim al-Amin (journalist for the Lebanese daily *al-Safir*), remarks made on the program *Files,* al-Manar Television, April 2, 2002.

Avi Jorisch

90. For more information on this group, see Reuven Paz, "The Attack of January 17, 2000, in Hadera," International Policy Institute for Counter-Terrorism, January 17, 2000; available online (www.ict.org.il/spotlight/comment.cfm?id=385). Since the beginning of the intifada, the group has used al-Manar as its mouthpiece when claiming responsibility for attacks. The group publicly announced its connection with Abu Musa's faction on November 1, 2000 ("Dissident Palestinian Faction Affirms Link with 'Clandestine Group,'" al-Manar Television, November 1, 2000, BBC Summary of World Broadcasts, November 3, 2000). Abu Fadi Hamad, the Abu Musa faction's general secretary and foreign relations head, visited al-Manar on November 4, 2000, where he met with Nayef Krayem and thanked him for the assistance that the station had provided to the intifada (information obtained from an Israeli military document dated October 22, 2002).

91. This organization is notorious for being featured on al-Manar taking credit for actions such as shooting at Israeli cars.

92. The Jerusalem Brigades began to appear on al-Manar in November 2000, taking responsibility for numerous attacks. Al-Manar was also the first television station to broadcast clips of artillery fire by PIJ activists against Israeli targets. A large number of high-ranking PIJ officials, including Secretary-General Ramadan Abdallah Shallah, have been interviewed on the station since the beginning of the intifada.

93. Since the intifada began, this organization has used al-Manar to claim responsibility for at least six attacks, four of which involved shelling the Jewish settlement of Netzarim in Gaza. The other two claims were for attacks that never took place. Apparently, Badr Brigades is a cover name for a Gaza-based Hizballah cell headed by Masoud Iyad. Iyad was a colonel in Force 17, the Palestinian presidential guard; other members of this force participated in his cell's terrorist activities as well. He was killed by Israeli forces on February 13, 2001.

94. Mathew Levitt, *Targeting Terror: U.S. Policy toward Middle Eastern State Sponsors and Terrorist Organizations,* Post–September 11 (Washington, D.C.: Washington Institute for Near East Policy, 2002), p. 113.

95. Hourani was arrested by Israeli forces in January 2004. Margot Dudkevitch, "Senior al-Aksa Brigades Terrorist Arrested," *Jerusalem Post* (online edition), January 7, 2004. Available online (www.jpost.com/servlet/Satellite?pagename=JPost/JPArticle/ShowFull&cid=1073448210095&p=1008596981749).

96. Lee Hockstader, "Arafat's Reach Limited among Militants: Angry Crowd Prevents Arrest of Journalist with Ties to Extremist Group," *Washington Post,* December 4, 2001.

97. Information obtained from an Israeli military document dated October 22, 2002.

98. Matthew Levitt, "Banning Hizballah Activity in Canada," *PolicyWatch* no. 698, Washington Institute for Near East Policy (January 6, 2003). The case in question was United States vs. Hammoud, no. 3:00CR147-MU (W.D. N.C.).

99. Mathew Levitt, interview by author, The Washington Institute for Near East Policy, Washington, D.C., November 12, 2003. For more information on the trial, see remarks by Kenneth Bell as summarized in Katherine Weitz, "Hizbollah Fundraising in the American Heartland," *PolicyWatch* no. 700, Washington Institute for Near East Policy (January 15, 2003).

100. Untitled article in *al-Safir* (Beirut), December 29, 1994.

101. Ali Dahir, interview, *al-Nahar* (Beirut), September 2, 1992.

102. John Lancaster, "Hezbollah Tunes In on Profits; Party's TV Station Airing U.S. Movies," *Washington Post,* June 19, 1995. Some of the foreign films and series were purchased in the United

Arab Emirates. See "Hezbollah's Voice of Light Radio Station not Licensed," *al-Nahar* (Beirut), July 25, 1997, BBC Summary of World Broadcasts, August 1, 1997.

103. Yoel Marcus, "The Pessimists Were Right," *Haaretz* (Tel Aviv), October 6, 2000.

104. It should be noted that debate persists regarding the circumstances of al-Dura's death. No conclusive proof has emerged determining whether the bullet that killed the boy was fired by Palestinians or Israelis.

105. Frank Furedi, "The Rumour Machine That Fills a Need," *Times Higher Education Supplement* (London), February 22, 2002.

106. "4000 'Israeli' Employees in WTC Absent the Day of the Attack," Daily Report, Islamic Resistance Support Organization, September 18, 2001. Available online (go to www.moqawama.tv/page2/f_report.htm and find the archives link; the article in question appears as part of the "Daily Report" for September 18, 2001). See also Terence Tao, "The Case of the Missing 4000 Israelis," self-published article, last updated August 8, 2003. Available online (www.nocturne.org/~terry/wtc_4000_Israeli.html).

107. Michael Dobbs, "Myths over Attacks on U.S. Swirl through Islamic World—Many Rumors Lay Blame on an Israeli Conspiracy," *Washington Post,* October 13, 2001. See also Musa Hawamidah, "Bin Laden's Admission," *al-Dustur* (Amman), December 30, 2001, BBC Monitoring of World Broadcasts, December 30, 2001.

108. Bryan Curtis, "4,000 Jews, 1 Lie—Tracking an Internet Hoax," Slate.com, October 5, 2001. Available online (http://slate.msn.com/?id=116813).

109. "Hezbollah Leader Says Resistance to Israel 'Will Never Stop,'" *El Mundo* (Madrid), December 18, 2001.

110. Lhuillery, "Hezbollah TV: Waging a Broadcasting War."

111. Andrew Muller, "We're Coming to Get You: The U.S. Says Hizbollah Is a Bunch of Terrorists Who Should Be Destroyed," *The Independent* (London), April 7, 2002.

112. Lhuillery, "Hezbollah TV: Waging a Broadcasting War."

113. Jacki Hugi, "The Voice of Quiet Thunder," *Maariv Sofshavua* supplement (in Hebrew), July 26, 2002.

PART 2

CONTENT ANALYSIS

CHAPTER 3

ANTI-AMERICAN PROPAGANDA

The United States is one of al-Manar's main targets. Hizballah views America as a terrorist state on the basis of Washington's policies toward the Arab world (specifically Iraq and Palestine), its strategic relationship with Israel, and its perceived efforts to bring about the downfall of Islam. Al-Manar is used to further that perception, attempting to win the hearts and minds of Arab and Muslim viewers by waging a powerful public relations campaign against the "Great Satan."[1]

Hizballah's characterization of the United States as a primary terrorist state was clearly delineated in a March 2002 speech commemorating the eighth night of the Shiite holiday of Ashura. Before thousands of spectators in Beirut and millions of al-Manar viewers, Sheikh Hassan Nasrallah, the organization's secretary-general, asserted:

> Today the main source of evil in this world, the main source of terrorism in this world, the central threat to international peace and to the economic development of the world, the main threat to the environment of this world, the main source of…killing and turmoil, and civil wars and regional wars in this world is the United States of America.…The American political discourse is to terrorize the countries of the world.…America is a beast in all meanings of the word. A beast that is hungry for power and hungry for blood."[2]

In another speech broadcast on al-Manar, Nasrallah stated, "Our enmity to the Great Satan is complete and unlimited.…Our echoing slogan will remain: Death to America!"[3] Similarly, Sheikh Hassan Izz al-Din, a member of Hizballah's Political Council and the party's director for media relations, contended, "America will fall just like the Romans and the British. While it now controls the world, this will change. We cannot accept American domination and American terrorist actions."[4]

Much of al-Manar's programming is skewed toward disseminating these views of the United States. On one program, for example, station guests maintained that Washington was using the events of September 11, 2001, "in order to implement plans already in place" against Islam and to "justify an ugly foreign policy...and U.S. military spending."[5] Other al-Manar guests have gone so far as to suggest that "the U.S. has become a possible theatre of war, wars of revenge."[6]

A POLICY OF OPPRESSION

According to al-Manar, the United States is not only a terrorist state, but also the world's chief oppressor. Many of the station's programs parade the circumstances of the birth of the United States as proof of its oppressor status, particularly its treatment of Native Americans and expropriation of their land.[7] These programs maintain that the United States has perpetuated such oppression throughout its history (e.g., importing "slaves from Africa and killing them in millions" and "dropping the atomic bomb" during World War II).[8] Most important, al-Manar officials emphasize that such oppression continues unabated. For example, Sheikh al-Din asserted that "the black population of America" is oppressed and "suffering at the hands of the American government." In this manner, Hizballah distorts American history to portray present-day U.S. foreign policy as a natural extension of the country's oppressive past. Even the tragic events of September 11 are depicted as a tool with which Washington can "deepen intervention in the region and expand its sphere of influence."[9]

Following up on the station's distorted depiction of U.S. history, al-Manar guests often warn viewers in Palestine and the Arab world that they will meet the same fate as the Native Americans if they do not rise up and resist the United States and its allies: "Look at the Indians. Where are they? They signed and look at their fate. Does Palestine, Jordan, Egypt want to sign as well? Do you want to share the same Indian fate?!"[10] Similarly, Nasrallah claimed, "If it was not for the bravery of the Palestinian people, America's solution for the Palestinian people would have been the same solution they had to their problem with the Red Indians, the original people of America."[11] According to another guest, the modern-day epitome of U.S. oppression—the U.S.-Zionist conspiracy—threatens to "penetrate into Palestine...and spread to Lebanon and the other Arab nations like a plague."[12]

During appearances on al-Manar, Hizballah officials often contend that the goal of current U.S. foreign policy is to "enslave the governments and people of the [Middle East] and steal their resources." Once the United States has attained this goal, it will "dispose of all who have helped her."[13] As Ayatollah Muhammad Hussein Fadlallah, regarded by many as Hizballah's spiritual leader, declared on one program, America intends to "confiscate people's liberties, strategic locations, natural resources, and economic markets."[14] Al-Manar has also featured footage of Iranian leaders (such as Supreme Leader Ali Khamenei and the late Ayatollah Ruhollah Khomeini) endorsing similar positions (see video clips 18 and 19).

The notion that the United States is a global oppressor is powerfully expressed in an al-Manar video that features an altered image of the Statue of Liberty (see video clip 20). The statue's head has been transformed into a skull with hollow eyes, her gown dripping in blood. Instead of a torch, she holds a sharp knife. A list of America's conflicts over the past fifty years is set to ominous-sounding music. Names such as Afghanistan, Korea, Lebanon, Vietnam, and Somalia are coupled with images of nuclear war, bloody massacres, and planes bombing targets. After asserting that the United States "has pried into the affairs of most countries in the world," the video ends with the slogan, "America owes blood to all of humanity."

REFERENCE VIDEO CLIPS
18, 19, 20, and 21

Indeed, al-Manar repeatedly airs rejectionist voices calling on Arab and Muslim leaders to "mobilize the energies of the [Muslim] nation to resist U.S.-Zionist terrorism."[15] This theme is highlighted in a video that features images from U.S. military actions in places such as Hiroshima, Korea, Afghanistan, and Baghdad (see video clip 21).[16] The video combines these images with footage from various Israeli military incidents. The video ends with a slogan calling for an end to U.S. and Israeli "crimes against humanity."

When speaking to Western audiences, both Hizballah and al-Manar officials claim to harbor no animosity toward the American people, instead directing their resentment toward U.S. foreign policy. According to al-Din, "We are not against the American people, but we oppose the American government's policies on our radio, television, and websites." Yet al-Manar prominently features programming in Arabic that expresses the opposite message; as Fadlallah argued, "The instincts of American people…are filled with hatred for the Arabs and Muslims and…are under the influence of the Zionist propaganda."[17]

Al-Manar frequently disseminates the view that the United States, being an oppressor, has no right to act "as a judge in the world" or to impose its "hegemony."[18] By extension, the United States has no right to label Hizballah a terrorist organization. As one station guest put it, "How dare they say that they are against terrorism and fighting against it?"[19] According to such thinking, the colonialist essence of the United States and Israel make them both terrorist states. Therefore, by violently opposing both U.S. foreign policy and the occupation of historic Palestine, Hizballah is actually fighting terrorism:

> Jihad, resistance, martyrdom—spiritually, culturally, politically—is actually removing terrorism. Humanity will not be blessed without removing their [America's] type of terrorism....We have to continue our jihad in all different types in order to save humanity from this [American] terrorist thinking.[20]

In an effort to explain U.S. opposition, al-Manar guest Muhammad Fanish, a member of Hizballah's parliamentary bloc, claimed that Washington had classified Hizballah as a terrorist organization because the party "is at war with Israel."[21] Failing to acknowledge the numerous other reasons why his organization had been placed on U.S. terrorism lists, he concluded that such a classification is the result of "Hizballah's resistance movement against Israel and its overt support of the intifada. Hizballah poses a threat to Israel, and [Americans] simply want to protect their best friend in the region." Similarly, in a May 24, 2002, speech broadcast on al-Manar, Nasrallah stated, "America knows she is lying when she says that Hizballah is a threat to U.S. national security."

U.S. LEADERS

Al-Manar programming often portrays U.S. leaders as evil, pernicious, and equivalent to Israel's leadership. In fact, its treatment of such leaders is literally inflammatory—just as the station shows images of American flags being burned and stepped on by demonstrators, it also highlights footage in which effigies of American leaders are burned.

The station is particularly hostile toward President George W. Bush, labeling him a "stupid and crazy person" and comparing him to Adolf Hitler.[22] One al-Manar video features images of

**REFERENCE VIDEO CLIPS
22 and 23**

Hitler and Bush side by side, making it look as though the two leaders are making the same salute, giving the same speeches, and perpetrating the same brutal massacres (see video clip 22). The video ends with the message—written onscreen in both Arabic and English—"History repeats itself."

In another video based on the theme "Beauty and the Beast," "beauty" is pictured as planet Earth from the perspective of space (see video clip 23). As the video progresses, President Bush—depicted as the "beast"—appears to be eating Earth with a knife and fork and using an American flag as a napkin. Soon thereafter, the background changes into a stream of tanks, fighter jets, and explosions moving out from behind the president.

Al-Manar also accuses Bush of waging war against "Islam as a belief" under the guise of the war on terror. The station's programming explicitly argues that the United States is, as Nasrallah asserted on March 14, 2002, waging a campaign to depict Islam as a "religion of terror, hate, destruction, evil, barbarism, a religion against peace, civilization, and modernity." According to Nasrallah, the United States regards the Quran as the "source of hate and terrorism." He pointed to Bush's comments about the war on terror being a "crusade" as sufficient proof of U.S. enmity. Nasrallah further warned viewers that the United States "stole our land in Palestine; now they are coming to destroy the essence of our religion." Similarly, in a November 23, 2002, speech on al-Manar, Nasrallah stated outright that he views the United States as "the enemy of this *umma* [community of believers]."

Al-Manar programming has also contended that "Christian Zionists are in charge of the American [i.e., Bush] administration."[23] The Arabic version of the term "Christian Zionists" is reserved for supposed right-wing Christian supporters of Israel who "misinterpret the holy Bible to justify the Zionist occupation of Palestine."[24] Al-Manar calls on its viewers to distinguish between "real Christians" and "Zionist Christians who use the cross, Jesus, and the Virgin Mary to mask their Zionism." On one program, for example, Lebanese minister of information Michel Semaha made the following arguments:

> American politics today is ruled, along with oil alliances and military industry alliances…by an extremist ideological alliance, an alliance between Likudist-Zionist extremism that exists in the Pentagon, the NSC [National Security Council], and the White House.…They are Christian Zionists, a movement that has nothing to do with the true church, whether Protestant or Catholic. Those people surrounded President Bush and took him ideologically and politically.[25]

Similarly, a Palestinian guest on al-Manar quipped, "We might even see that the headquarters of the Israeli chiefs of staff will be in the White House someday. Those Jewish-Likudist-Zionists in the administration—[Paul] Wolfowitz, [Richard] Perle, and others—are worse than [Binyamin] Netanyahu and other Israeli Likudists."[26] Another guest emphasized that Americans do not come to the region to "solve the problems" but rather to "give the Israelis more time to continue their destruction of Palestinian areas."[27]

Various al-Manar videos underscore these points. In one video, a large coin spins amid scenes of fire and carnage (see video clip 10). Images of President Bush and Prime Minister Ariel Sharon appear on different sides of this coin; below, the slogan "two faces, one terrorism" appears.[28]

REFERENCE VIDEO CLIP
10

A similar video features images of dead bodies and planes bombing their targets, interspersed with footage of U.S. and Israeli leaders (see video clip 24). Bush and Sharon are

REFERENCE VIDEO CLIPS
24 and 25

shown sitting together, and Bush declares, "I believe he [Sharon] has shown patience, and this is my opportunity to once again look him in the eye and tell him he's got no better friend than the United States." Bush's statement is immediately followed by English text that reads, "Who committed the murder?? Israeli hands or American arms[?]"

Yet another video in this vein couples images of Bush and Sharon chatting amiably with violent images from various notable events linked with the Israeli prime minister (e.g., the 1982 massacres in the Palestinian refugee camps of Sabra and Shatila) (see video clip 25). Throughout the video, White House Press Secretary Ari Fleischer is shown saying, "The president believes that Ariel Sharon is a man of peace." The video ends with text in English and Arabic reading, "Peace on [*sic*] the American Way."

THE U.S.-ISRAELI STRATEGIC ALLIANCE AND THE QUESTION OF PALESTINE

In general, al-Manar portrays the strategic alliance between Israel and the United States as an unshakable, natural bond between two oppressors. Station guests have told viewers that Washington's main objective in the region is to "give the green light to the Zionist entity to do as it pleases regarding the Palestinian people, the intifada, and to resistance."[29] According to this view, the United States wants to pressure Palestinians and Arabs into accepting "frivolous negotiations" with the Israelis that will achieve "nothing for the Palestinian people."

REFERENCE VIDEO CLIP
26

Moreover, in a series of videos titled *Veto*, al-Manar informs viewers that the United States has vetoed thirty-seven different UN proposals meant to "protect Palestinian civilians and Arab rights" (see video clip 26). Each of these videos lists one or more of the thirty-seven decisions and then shows an American flag veto stamp crashing down on the proposal. Such scenes are often followed by footage of people wailing and a sarcastic slogan at the bottom of the screen that reads, "Thank you, America."

Al-Manar guests also depict the United States as a biased negotiator in the Arab-Israeli conflict. As one guest put it, "We will not under any circumstances submit to a peace proposal by America" because U.S. policy advocates a Palestinian state that "fits the interests of Israel."[30] This same guest encouraged viewers to "adopt a strategy of complete liberation" and declared a willingness "to pay the price for such a strategy."

Whereas the United States is depicted as the guardian of Israeli interests, al-Manar often portrays Israelis as the "foot soldiers of our true and original enemy, [the American] Satan."[31] As Israel's primary sponsor, the United States is responsible for the terror that Israel has inflicted on the region. By not supporting a Palestinian state with all of Jerusalem as its capital or allowing refugees to return to all of historic Palestine, the United States aims to force Palestinians "to accept nothing but crumbs, to accept a small fraction of their historical rights."[32]

Other al-Manar programs explicitly warn viewers that "Zionist Jews or American Zionists" wish to destroy the al-Aqsa Mosque in Jerusalem. For example, in a speech broadcast on November 29, 2002, Nasrallah claimed that the chances of the mosque being destroyed, "which Talmudic Zionists are determined to do, is exceptionally great today when 'Christian Zionists' are in charge in the American [i.e. Bush] administration." At the same time, he warned, anyone attempting to carry out such an act "will find our blood erupting like volcanoes from under his feet. This is the case for whoever the aggressor might be, be [he] a Zionist Jew or an American Zionist."

Al-Manar also provides forums for viewers to call in and express similarly extreme militant views. For example, one Bahraini caller named Galal offered the following remarks:

> Peace be upon you. I salute the fighters in Palestine. We are with you and our hearts are with you. We must praise God, and there is no God but God. May God punish America and Israel. May God punish those Arab traitors with them. May God punish the Jews and the Zionists, and *in sha' Allah* we will liberate Jerusalem soon. [Here the program host answers "in *sha' Allah*," or "if God wills it."] *In sha' Allah* we will pray in Jerusalem soon. May God destroy America. [The host again answers *"in sha' Allah"*] May God destroy the Arab traitors.[33]

Such remarks demonstrate how closely the United States and Israel are paired in Hizballah's mindset.

THE IRAQI FRONT

Since March 2003, when the U.S.-led campaign in Iraq began, Hizballah has openly called for acts of violence against Americans there. Indeed, Hizballah's stance is strikingly similar to al-Qaeda's declared goal of driving U.S. forces out of the Middle East. Accordingly, al-Manar propaganda has expanded to include vitriolic condemnation of the U.S. role in Iraq.

As the war became imminent, al-Manar devoted more airtime to the crisis and directed increasingly violent language toward the United States. A week before the invasion began, Nasrallah declared,

REFERENCE VIDEO CLIP
27

Do not expect the people of this region to receive you with flowers and basil, rice and perfume. Rather, the people will meet you with rifles, with blood and arms, with martyrdom and suicide operations. Today, our region may be filled with hundreds of thousands of American troops and fleets. Our slogan was, our slogan is still today, and our slogan will remain: 'Death to America!'" (see video clip 27)

With the commencement of war, al-Manar featured a new series of powerful videos and programs geared toward an already agitated audience. In one video, images of American firepower (e.g., aircraft carriers; Tomahawk missiles landing in Baghdad) and of dead Iraqi children and other civilians are coupled with footage of Secretary of Defense Donald Rumsfeld asserting, "Weapons that are being used today have a degree of precision that no one ever dreamt of" (see video clip 28). The video ends with the image of crosshairs on a wounded child and a slogan that reads, "Indeed…very precise!" Other videos and programs offer similar images as well as slogans such as "American aggression against Iraq" (see video clip 29) and "Shake

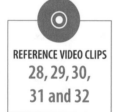

REFERENCE VIDEO CLIPS
28, 29, 30,
31 and 32

the walls of aggression" (see video clip 30). Yet another video features grotesque images of Iraqi death and destruction coupled with a speech in which President Bush asserts, "When the war in Iraq is won, all that have joined this cause will be able to say to the Iraqi people, we were proud to fight for your freedom" (see video clip 31). The video ends with a graphic that reads, "Freedom: the American way."

Al-Manar has aired similarly inflammatory programming touching on key events in the postwar period. For example, one video begins as a seemingly innocent English-language advertisement for the 2004 film *The Passion of the Christ,* showing footage of the movie interspersed with the phrases "No Mercy" and "No Compassion" (see video clip 32). At the end of the video, however, al-Manar alters the title of the film to read "The Passion of the Iraqis," juxtaposing it with an image from the Abu Ghraib prison torture scandal.

In addition to inciting anger toward the U.S. presence in Iraq, al-Manar has depicted the war and its aftermath as a further indication that the United States "is seeking to assert total Zionist hegemony in the region." As one correspondent claimed,

As the aggression continues, the brave resistance will continue. The brave Iraqi people know that if they give up, they won't only be giving up Iraq, but also giving up Palestine....For [the] aggression, experts agree, symbolizes the highest level of American-Zionist strategic cooperation. This is what the Zionists prove by claiming that they are the first and only beneficiaries of a war on Iraq.[34]

Viewers are even warned that the United States is willing and able to use weapons of mass destruction (WMD) in order to achieve its goals in Iraq and elsewhere in the Arab world. In one program broadcast in April 2003, Husni al-Hayik, labeled a "specialist on Israeli weapons of mass destruction," asserted,

America might use WMD and has used [them] many times before....There are Torah-based reasons for many Americans to use WMD....Therefore, it is essential that there be a world and Arab movement against this Torah-based project. This is a Torah-based plan to finish all Islam.

Al-Manar has also broadcast explicit calls for acts of resistance against U.S. forces in Iraq. One video lambastes U.S. troops in Iraq with the following lyrics: "Down with the mother of terrorism! America threatens in vain, an occupying army of invaders. Nothing remains but rifles and suicide bombers" (see video clip 33). The video ends with an image of a suicide bomber's belt detonating.

REFERENCE VIDEO CLIP
33

In general, al-Manar propaganda incites violence and hatred toward Americans in the region at a time when the lives of U.S. military personnel are already on the line. Because freedom of speech and freedom of the press are fundamental rights in the United States, Washington has attempted to be sensitive in its efforts to coax foreign governments into controlling the media in their own countries. Now is a time of war, however. As Deputy Secretary of Defense Paul Wolfowitz stated, "What I am complaining of are false reporting and very biased reporting that [have] the effect of inciting violence against our troops, and these governments should stop and realize that this is not a game, that they are endangering the lives of American troops."[35] Such complaints are readily applicable to the types of programming featured on al-Manar.

NOTES

1. Hassan Nasrallah, speech broadcast on al-Manar Television, September 27, 2002.

2. Hassan Nasrallah, speech broadcast on al-Manar Television, March 20, 2002.

3. Nasrallah speech, September 27, 2002.

4. Unless otherwise indicated, all quotes attributed to al-Manar and Hizballah personnel were obtained from the individuals in question during interviews conducted at the Beirut station on June 27–28, 2002. The titles attributed to these personnel represent the positions they held at the time of the interviews.

5. Maan Bashour (president of the Society of Popular Committees and Associations, a private Lebanese political organization), remarks made on the program *What's Next?*, al-Manar Television, March 13, 2002.

6. Diyaa Rashwan (research fellow at the al-Ahram Center for Strategic Studies), remarks made on the program *What's Next?*, al-Manar Television, March 13, 2002. During this same episode, the host of the program categorized the United States as an enemy of Islam.

7. Nasrallah speech, March 20, 2002. Identical sentiments were expressed by station guest Sheikh Babil al-Halbawi, imam of the al-Sayida Rikiyya Mosque in Damascus, during an episode of the program *Files,* al-Manar Television, April 4, 2002.

8. Al-Halbawi, *Files.*

9. Remarks made by program host, *What's Next?*, al-Manar Television, March 13, 2002.

10. Leith Shbeilat (head of the anti-Zionist society in Jordan), remarks made on the program *Terrorists,* al-Manar Television, March 6, 2002. Nasrallah echoed these sentiments in his March 20, 2002, speech broadcast on al-Manar.

11. Nasrallah speech, March 20, 2002.

12. Al-Halbawi, *Files.*

13 Nasrallah speech, September 27, 2002.

14. "Lebanese Shi'i Leader Says USA Wants to 'Subordinate the Entire World,'" al-Manar Television, February 1, 2002, Financial Times Information, Global News Wire, February 1, 2002.

15. "Hamas Source Says President Bush's 'Threats' Will Not Intimidate Movement," al-Manar Television, January 31, 2002, BBC Summary of World Broadcasts, January 31, 2002.

16. The Baghdad incident highlighted in this video is the U.S. aerial bombing of the Amiriya shelter in February 1991, which resulted in the deaths of 403 civilians. "Victims of the US and British Air Raids in Iraq," ArabicNews.com, February 14, 2000. Available online (www.arabicnews.com/ansub/Daily/Day/000214/2000021415.html).

17. "Lebanese Shi'i Leader Says USA Wants to 'Subordinate the Entire World.'"

18. "Hamas Source Says President Bush's 'Threats' Will Not Intimidate Movement."

19. Al-Halbawi, *Files.* Nasrallah echoed these sentiments in his March 20, 2002, speech broadcast on al-Manar.

20. Al-Halbawi, *Files.*

21. Muhammad Fanish, remarks made on the program *News of the Hour,* al-Manar Television, January 18, 2002.

22. Hassan Nasrallah, speech broadcast on al-Manar Television, May 24, 2002.

23. Hassan Nasrallah, speech broadcast on al-Manar Television, November 29, 2002. See also Badih Chayban, "Nasrallah Alleges 'Christian Zionist' Plot," *Daily Star* (Beirut), October 23, 2002.

24. Archbishop Attalah Hana (spokesman for "the Orthodox Church in al-Quds [Jerusalem] and the Palestinian Territories"), remarks made on the program *News of the Hour,* al-Manar Television, March 15, 2002.

25. Michel Semaha, remarks made on the program *What's Next?,* al-Manar Television, April 20, 2003.

26. Mounir Shafeeq, remarks made on the program *American Aggression,* al-Manar Television, March 24, 2003.

27. Hussein al-Haj Hasan (member of the Lebanese parliament who represents the Hizballah bloc), remarks made on the program *Files,* al-Manar Television, April 13, 2002.

28. See also "Lebanon's Hezbollah TV Associates U.S., Israeli Leaders with Terrorism," al-Manar Television, April 27, 2002, BBC Summary of World Broadcasts, April 29, 2002.

29. Ismail Haniya (Hamas leader), remarks made on the program *Files,* al-Manar Television, April 2, 2002.

30. Al-Halbawi, *Files.*

31. Hassan Nasrallah, speech broadcast on al-Manar Television, March 19, 2002.

32. Haniya, *Files.* Nasrallah used very similar language in a speech broadcast on al-Manar on March 17, 2002 (see chapter 4).

33. Remarks made on the program *Files,* al-Manar Television, April 4, 2002.

34. Remarks made on the program *The Aftermath Report,* al-Manar Television, March 24, 2003.

35. "'False Reporting' in Arab Media Incites Anti-US Violence in Iraq," Agence France Presse, July 27, 2003.

CHAPTER 4

DESTRUCTION OF ISRAEL

Just as Hizballah considers the United States the world's chief oppressor, it also equates Zionism with terrorism. Israel is viewed as having been born at the expense of the Palestinian people, and its very existence is deemed illegitimate. Hizballah therefore encourages Arabs and Muslims to unite behind the cause of obliterating Israel. Members of Hizballah, academics, philosophers, religious leaders (Sunni and Shiite alike), and community leaders are paraded on al-Manar to support this outlook, and many of the station's videos serve this same purpose (see video clip 34).

In August 2000, Hizballah secretary-general Hassan Nasrallah was shown on al-Manar stating, "Any Islamic movement or national Arab movement has to face up to the Zionist plan and work to liberate all territory and Palestine from the sea to the river."[1] Similarly, al-Manar

REFERENCE VIDEO CLIPS
34 and 35

general manager and chairman of the board Nayef Krayem asserted, "Al-Manar TV supports all activities having to do with removing occupation and racism that Israel is carrying out. For us, the Zionist entity represents occupation and racism, and we support the destruction of occupation and racism."[2]

Hizballah's goal of destroying Israel is clearly expressed in two videos titled "Death to Israel" (Al-mawtu li israil) and "Rise Up, Rise Up, You Arab" (Inhad, inhad, ya ayyuha l-Araby). The former features footage of the intifada, suicide bombers, the aftermath of terrorist attacks, and the Dome of the Rock, with repeated chants of "Death to Israel" (see video clip 35). The video also shows Nasrallah stating:

> We have a faith in which there is no doubt, and a commitment in which there is no hesitation. And our commitment is to the resistance, to its rifles, its bullets, and the blood of

its mujahedin. Death to Israel!…No one has the right to give up a single grain of sand from the land of Palestine, and no one has the right to erase even one single letter from the name of Palestine.…Israel is utterly null and void, and it's a raping, deviant, occupying, terrorist, cancerous entity that has no legitimacy or legality at all, and never will.

Lyrics sung throughout the video include the following:

Write in running blood: Death! Death! Death to Israel! And cause with the exploding body death! death! death to Israel!…From the wounds of al-Dura, al-Ayash, and Izz al-Din,[3] create days of victory, and challenge the occupiers. From the land of angry Jerusalem, drive out the raping occupier. Expel from your house that one, that Zionist humiliated.…Strike them with the stone, slingshot, and knife. Chase them day and night, for the will is strong.…Like an erupting volcano, shake the structure of the treacherous.…Do not mind the heavy equipment and weapons of the soldiers.…Have no mercy on the army of aggression, those wearing the garb of the military and of settlement.

Nasrallah also appears in the second video, first released on al-Manar's main website (see video clip 36). In it, he challenges fellow Arabs to account for what they have personally done to liberate Palestine and Jerusalem. Population figures for each Arab country are listed, and the

REFERENCE VIDEO CLIP
36

video ends with big letters that read, "Population of the Arab world: 300 million Arabs. Occupied Palestine: 5 million Jews. What are you waiting for?" The clear message to viewers is that the Arab world should encounter no difficulty in destroying Israel through sheer numbers alone.

Other religious figures, Christian and Muslim alike, have advocated similar views on al-Manar. On one program, Archbishop Attalah Hana, spokesman for the Orthodox Church of Jerusalem, called on the Arab League to support Palestinians: "We need political and economic support.…We expect Arab support in all the means and ways available, including military support."[4] Indeed, Hizballah unequivocally supports military force to destroy Israel. According to Hussein al-Haj Hasan, one of the organization's representatives in the Lebanese parliament, "Arab armies are to be ready…to give themselves over for the Palestinian cause."[5]

Hence, when certain al-Manar guests use the word "peace" with regard to Israel, they clearly are not referring to normal and friendly relations; they are, in fact, calling for the destruction of Israel. For example, Sheikh Taha al-Sabounji, the head mufti of northern Lebanon, based in Tripoli, declared the following:

But what they [Americans] refer to as peace between us and Israel, that we reject. We reject this falsehood. We reject what Bush just said half an hour ago, that Israel has to withdraw from the lands it reoccupied. It is another falsehood or lie in the sum of falsehood and lies that are being disseminated in order to give Israel enough time to accomplish the worst of violations. We call for immediate action....We need to dismantle this reality, shed the shackles....This Palestinian intifada is not going to end anytime soon....This problem will not be solved even if the Palestinians get a state.[6]

According to al-Sabounji, only when the Arab world adopts a "strategy of liberation in all its forms" will the United States "say yes to the Arabs and Muslims. Then, the Jews will feel fear [and] horror in their hearts—the horror we feel right now." Similarly, other al-Manar guests maintain that they cannot work with any of Israel's leaders in achieving their vision of "peace": "Whether it was Sharon or Barak or Peres or Rabin...a settlement or a peace deal is not our piece of cake."[7] In other words, Hizballah and its supporters are not interested in a peace agreement with any of Israel's leaders, be they on the left wing or the right. As Abdullah al-Makhlafi, secretary-general of the Nasserite Union Coalition in Yemen, declared, "The intifada is eternal until the day of liberation"[8] (see video clip 37).

REFERENCE VIDEO CLIP
37

Not surprisingly, then, al-Manar guests such as al-Sabounji encourage viewers—Arab Muslims and Arab Christians alike—to form an alliance and fight both Israel and world Jewry:

Judaism is a project against all humanity. It is about time the world understands this. Those who are fighting Israel are not just defending themselves; they are defending the whole world. They are protecting all the future generations of humanity. If they don't believe this, then they should read in the Jewish books what is written about Islam, Christianity, about Jesus and Muhammad. It's our job as Muslims to call upon the Christian world to rise up and become aware of what the Jews are doing....There is no such thing as Zionism....There is only Judaism....Zionism is a legend, a myth. These are the people [who] killed Muslims, Christians, and the prophets....Even the White House is ruled by Zionists and Jews—this despite the fact that America is a Christian country.[9]

Nasrallah underscored this same theme in remarks excerpted in an al-Manar video in which he called for a "Christian-Muslim alliance to confront those who show aggression toward

Moses, Jesus, and Muhammad" (see video clip 38). Elsewhere, Nasrallah stated, "If they [Jews] all gather in Israel, it will save us the trouble of going after them worldwide."[10]

REFERENCE VIDEO CLIP
38

Al-Manar also has an entire talk show, *The Spider's House,* dedicated to highlighting "the weaknesses of the 'Zionist Entity'" and to examining various strategies for destroying Israel (see appendix). Moreover, in other programs, guests such as Ismail Haniya, a Hamas leader, warn viewers that "the Zionist project, this cancer, will spread to the other Arab and Islamic states" if Israel is not defeated militarily.[11] Indeed, al-Manar argues that Palestine is the last line of defense in protecting the Arab and Muslim worlds from an ideology and culture that will infect the region with unspeakable evil. As Haniya put it, Arabs and Muslims must "persevere and unite" while supporting the intifada.

ZIONISM AS TERRORISM

Al-Manar's managers, anchors, producers, and station guests repeatedly question why—in the words of one Hizballah representative in the Lebanese parliament—America "fails to acknowledge that Zionist aggression is terrorism."[12] Instead, Washington "sees only Hizballah, always turning a deaf ear to Zionist entity aggression." Station guests depict this "Zionist entity" as an example of barbarism,[13] responsible for killing "doctors, nurses, the elderly, and the priests."[14] Indeed, all Zionists are deemed "racists and terrorists"[15] (see video clips 3 and 39). As Hashem Safi al-Din, head of Hizballah's steering committee, maintained, "The main pillar of the Zionist project is to impose a state based on terror in the region....The Zionist entity uses terror, murder, massacres, and treason with the explicit aim of oppressing the region. It is for this reason that we consider Zionism terrorism."[16] Zionism is even characterized as "Fascism that is equivalent to Hitler's final solution."[17]

REFERENCE VIDEO CLIPS
3, 39 and 40

One stated goal of al-Manar, therefore, is to "uncover" Israel's "terrorist operations" against the Palestinians, the Lebanese, and the broader Arab world. According to Muhammad Afif (identified on one program as a media advisor to Nasrallah), Western media, especially in the United States and Israel, have rewritten the facts of history to reflect "nothing but lies."[18] Therefore, al-Manar programming has adopted the explicit objective of revealing "the many lies of the Zionist entity in an appropriate and lucid manner" and of uncovering the "true picture of the Zionists' doings." Al-Manar encourages its Palestinian viewers to participate in this process, soliciting photographs that "expose the world to the brutality and aggression of the Zionist occupation army" (see video clip 40).

One al-Manar program—the half-hour weekly series *Terrorists* (Irhabiyyun)—is dedicated entirely to proving that Zionism is synonymous with terrorism. It often features anonymous narrators speaking over gory footage depicting dead children, wounded Arab civilians covered with blood, children lying in hospital beds, adults lying in coffins, Israeli military operations, burned Arab homes, destroyed mosques, torn copies of the Quran, religious Jews walking on the Temple Mount, and Palestinian funeral processions. Muhammad Husseini, the supervisor of *Terrorists,* claimed that the show's staff had to "dig deep into history books, newspapers, and interviews with families of victims and important officials who lived these sorrowful events" in order to uncover all of the "hidden historical facts." According to Husseini, his program alone has documented more than 700 examples of Zionist terrorism.[19]

In another episode of *Terrorists,* the narrator stated, "Zionist criminal behavior primarily targets Palestinians but does not exclude other Arabs."[20] Lebanon has "suffered the most at the hands of the Zionists, after the Palestinians, of course."[21] In a clear misrepresentation, a January 2002 episode asserted, "There has not been a day in the last fifty years that southern Lebanon has not been subjected to Zionist shelling."[22] Another episode claimed that Israel "has been terrorizing the region for 103 years."[23]

Every episode of *Terrorists* begins and ends in much the same fashion. Pictures of many of Israel's leading figures are featured, including Ben Gurion, Golda Meir, Zeev Jabotinsky, Theodor Herzl, Ehud Barak, Yitzhak Rabin, Yitzhak Shamir, and Binyamin Netanyahu. The pictures are followed by a slogan written in Arabic and in Hebrew: "Terrorists." This in turn is followed by a few lines attributed to the Jewish book of "Ishaya" in the "Zionist Talmud": "When you enter a village, stab those you encounter, kill with a sword those you capture, pulverize children on sight, take homes by force, and rape the women."[24] This misrepresented passage is apparently meant to show viewers that Jews are commanded by their religion and their leaders to commit such acts.

Each week, *Terrorists* painstakingly details Israeli military operations and the "atrocities" committed therein. The aforementioned gory footage is featured alongside sometimes excruciatingly long eyewitness interviews with crying children, distraught senior citizens, and others wounded in Israeli operations. The show interviews "people who have seen it all, lived it all, and who can paint an accurate picture of history."[25] Finally, each episode of *Terrorists* ends with a segment called "The Book of Zionist Crimes," a summary of Israeli military operations.

Avi Jorisch

JUSTIFYING AND INCITING PALESTINIAN VIOLENCE

As described in chapter 1, Hizballah and al-Manar view all Israelis as "occupiers." Accordingly, they do not regard any act of "resistance" against Israel as terrorism. Al-Manar uses this sort of reasoning to justify and encourage Palestinian violence against Israeli soldiers and civilians alike.

For example, Hizballah argues that all Israelis are legitimate targets because they are required to serve in the military (whether actively or as reservists). As Lebanese minister of information Michel Semaha stated on al-Manar, "Civilians are reservists who go and massacre Palestinians in the Jenin refugee camp....How can we make this distinction when…these 'civilians' are all reservists, thus potential 'Arab killers?'"[26] Ibrahim Musawi, the station's English-language editor-in-chief, went so far as to claim that "even [Jewish] schoolchildren have guns under their desks."

Such views are used to incite Palestinian violence at the popular level, in part by casting the Palestinian people as heroic underdogs facing a powerful, brutal enemy. Videos with titles such as "Jerusalem, We Are Coming" (Ya al-Quds inana qadimoun), "We Are a Volcano That Exploded" (Nahnu burkan tafajar), and "The Present Dies If You Are Not Enraged" (Mat al-hadhir in lam taghdhib) feature images from Palestinian demonstrations, including considerable gunfire (both into the air and aimed at Israeli soldiers); burning Israeli flags; children and women throwing stones; visibly angry crowds shaking their fists toward the sky and chanting slogans; signs declaring Israel's illegitimacy; militants with mock bombs attached to their bodies and sheets covering their heads; Palestinians of all ages throwing Molotov cocktails and burning tires at Israeli military posts; Israeli military vehicles engulfed in flames; and burning effigies of Israeli leaders.

Another video titled "I Am Coming Out, My Enemy" (Tal'alak ya adwi tal'a) includes the following lyrics: "I am coming out, my enemy, out of every house, street, and alley. This is our war, the war of the street. I am coming out; I am coming out." The song is accompanied by the beat of a distinctly Palestinian national folk dance, the Dabkeh, along with footage of Palestinians climbing up Jerusalem's walls, light poles, and tall buildings to raise the Palestinian flag.

Al-Manar programming also counsels the Palestinians to be patient with regard to the intifada, insisting that more time is needed to combat the Zionists (see video clip 41). According to Nasrallah, negotiations with Israel have yielded nothing, and violent resistance has

REFERENCE VIDEO CLIP

41

become the most effective means of realizing the establishment of a Palestinian state:

The Palestinian resistance has achieved an impact on the pillars of this entity Israel in two years that all the Arabs have not achieved in the past fifty years. Give the resistance some time. Why are you rushing it? Why are you saying it has failed and is making people despair? What have you achieved? We witnessed ten years of negotiations, humiliation, concessions, conditions, and counterconditions, and what did we achieve? Therefore, no one should pass judgment on this issue. I would like to see which people in the world have liberated their land in one or two years. The nature of the popular resistance is that it needs time. Give it time.[27]

RALLYING ARABS AND MUSLIMS

As discussed in chapter 2, al-Manar has also attempted to rally the wider and Arab and Muslim worlds around its anti-Israel message. Many of these efforts are aimed at taking citizens and governments alike to task for failing to fully support the Palestinians.[28] In addition to supporting the Palestinian cause on its own merits, al-Manar depicts the Israeli-Palestinian conflict as a key part of a larger effort to halt the "cancer" of Zionism. As Hamas leader Ismail Haniya asserted, the Palestinians are

> the head of the spear in this effort to combat the Zionist project....We are asking from the Arab world and Palestinians at...the formal and official level and also at the popular level...to consolidate this project of combating Zionism in order to benefit the whole Arab and Islamic world....This is why it is the responsibility of the whole Arab world to support this intifada and to give it all its support on all levels for the sake of [protecting] the whole Arab peoples.[29]

The host of one al-Manar program offered a similarly broad perspective on the importance of supporting the Palestinians and fighting Israel:

> Jihad leads to Arab and Islamic unity, and it nourishes the Palestinian cause. It is the path of life, pride, and dignity. And what our Palestinian brothers live today highlights the need for all kinds of jihad: political, military, financial, and cultural jihad. Our jihad against Israel is in defense of humanity and the civilized world. Resistance in Lebanon and in the beloved Palestine is an obligation for the Arab and Islamic world. Lastly, the Islamic resistance in Lebanon was the key that awakened the Arab and Islamic masses. The martyrs of the intifada are heroes. God bless the martyrs and their families, and may God give them more strength.[30]

In light of these views, al-Manar programming encourages Arabs and Muslims throughout the world to become more active in the struggle against Israel. As described in chapter 2, program guests call for demonstrations "every day, day after day, especially in Jordan and Egypt,"[31] even if such action brings the region to a state of "chaos."[32] Al-Manar posts the time and place of worldwide protests during commercial breaks (see video clip 42).

REFERENCE VIDEO CLIP
42

As for Arab and Muslim governments, al-Manar guests implore such regimes to desist from normalizing relations or signing peace agreements with Israel, to close down U.S. and Israeli embassies,[33] and to provide Palestinians with military support.[34] As Haniya stated, "It is not possible or logical for the Arab world to continue talking to Israel with all these massacres and killing in the background and Zionist aggressions."[35]

Al-Manar programming suggests that Arab governments have largely failed in their responsibilities toward the Palestinians. In fact, Hizballah regards many of these governments as lackeys of the West.[36] Hizballah's antagonism toward Arab regimes stems primarily from its perception that the Palestinians have been forced to accept illegitimate peace concessions. These regimes are accused of repeatedly putting forth proposals to the "illegitimate" state of Israel on behalf of the Palestinians. Adding insult to injury, such proposals have asked for only a fraction of the land in historic Palestine. Therefore, Hizballah demands that Arab governments cease instructing Palestinians to "sacrifice their land, history, pride, and integrity and accept crumbs."[37]

Other al-Manar programs include more threatening overtones. For example, during the April 10, 2002, episode of the talk show *Files* (Milafat), one caller suggested bringing down Arab regimes through violent means, including assassination, if they do not support the Palestinians against Israel: "One day there will be another Islamabuli[38] in Egypt, or Jordan, or elsewhere to avenge what these traitors have done." Al-Manar underscores this political message with religious implications. For example, Nasrallah threatened Arab leaders with the consequences they will face on the day of judgment, when they will be asked,

> Why did you collaborate? Why did you go quietly? Why did you get weak? Why didn't you offer your support [to the Palestinians]? Why did you allow them to call the resistance 'terrorism' and the resistance fighters 'terrorists'? Why didn't you help those seeking your help?[39]

In upbraiding those who pay only lip service to the Palestinian fight against Israel, al-Manar often invokes notions of Arab solidarity and duty. In a video titled

"My People on the [West] Bank, I am Coming" (Ya sh'abi fi al-dafa qadem), Nasrallah stated,

> We insist on standing side by side with our people in Palestine because our moral, ethical, and historical obligation demands that we do so. We do not shy away from our responsibility to shoulder our part of that confrontation....Every honorable Arab is with them in that battle.

He expressed similar sentiments in the video "God Is Greater Than the Aggressor's Might" (Allahu akbar fawwq kayd al-m'utadi): "Every Arab and Muslim knows that every grain of Palestinian sand is worth dying for."

As mentioned previously, one of the poster children calling Arabs and Muslims to action against Israel is Muhammad al-Dura, a Palestinian boy who was shot and killed during an Israeli-Palestinian clash in September 2000, during the first days of the intifada. Excruciating footage of al-Dura's death, which many in the region regard as deliberate murder on Israel's part, caused widespread outrage throughout the Arab world and came to symbolize the Palestinian struggle. Al-Manar has readily exploited this symbolism, placing images of the boy's death in many of its programs and propaganda videos. For example, lyrics to the video "Palestine's Dura"[40] include the following:

> Brother, run. I warn you not to trip; hide behind the barrel....Father, I wanted Jerusalem to be free; protect me in your arms. Father...is scooping me out with a smile on his face....Father, do not show pain, for now I am comfortable.[41]

Such videos play a key role in Hizballah's attempt to disseminate its rejectionist ideology to broader Arab and Muslim communities. By broadcasting this brand of militant rhetoric, al-Manar incites further violence and widens the gap between Israelis and Palestinians, thereby making a viable solution to the conflict even more elusive.

DESTRUCTION THROUGH DEMOGRAPHY

Al-Manar programs often assert that Arabs can effectively ensure Israel's obliteration through the Palestinian "human nuclear bomb." As one program guest asserted, "The demographic threat is the biggest weapon in our arsenal."[42] According to him, the Arab-Israeli conflict is a "conflict of presence":

It is either us [Arabs] or them [Jews] who can physically be present in the land of Palestine....Our entire people know that this land is Palestine from [the Mediterranean] Ocean to the Jordan River. This is a struggle for removal. This is an existential struggle....There has to be a realization among the different factions of Palestinian leadership [that] this is a conflict about existence and not about borders."

Accordingly, Hizballah and al-Manar encourage Palestinians residing in the West Bank and Gaza to increase their birthrate.

In general, the rate of natural population growth among Arabs in the Middle East hovers at 3.5 percent, one of the highest rates in the world. Thus, demographers estimate that the region's Arab population will double within the next twenty to twenty-five years.[43] Because of this exponentially increasing birthrate, al-Manar programming often expresses confidence that "Israel will be wiped off the face of the planet in, at most, two generations."[44] Hizballah hopes to compound the forthcoming demographic shift by demanding that the international community give the Palestinian diaspora the "right of return" to all of historic Palestine (see video clip 43).

REFERENCE VIDEO CLIP
43

Al-Manar's efforts to highlight demography are aimed at Arab Israelis as well. For example, the station has highlighted statistics indicating that Jews will eventually constitute a minority in the area west of the Jordan River.[45] From al-Manar's perspective, a dramatic increase in the Arab Israeli population could play a significant role in facilitating this trend.

Al-Manar also encourages Arab Israeli viewers to use their democratic rights to vote Israeli Jews out of power.[46] For example, if all Arab Israelis had voted for the same party in the 2000 elections—to be sure, an unlikely scenario—they would have garnered as many as 24 of the Knesset's 120 seats. Citing the Israeli Bureau of Statistics, the February 27, 2002, episode of *The Spider's House* pointed out that Arab Israelis will constitute 25 percent of the Israeli population by 2020, representing a potential electoral power of thirty Knesset seats.

The message of such statistical work is clear: one of the ways to destroy Israel is through its own political system. By this logic, democratic rights are merely a means to an end. According to one researcher featured on the program,

Today the Arab Israelis number 20 percent. In 2020, they will be at least 30 percent, if not 35 or 40 percent, and this number is not going to stop growing. Indeed, these people's sense of nationalism is heightening, and they are already demanding their rights. It will be difficult for a government to inflict racist policies on them as they are growing larger.[47]

In fact, racism based on demographics is a frequent theme of *The Spider's House.* For example, this same researcher compared Israel to South Africa, labeling it an "inherently racist and apartheid [state] in every sense of the word" due to its treatment of Arab Israelis (see video clips 44 and 45). Other guests on *The Spider's House*

REFERENCE VIDEO CLIPS
44 and 45

and similar programs contend that Israel will eventually collapse as a result of this perceived racism. One such guest, identified as an "expert" in "Zionist affairs," asserted, "Any system that classified 20 percent of its population as second-class citizens is bound to fail...sooner or later."[48] Another guest, identified as a "researcher in refugee affairs," stated, "This entity, by definition of what it stands for, is a racist entity, and just like apartheid fell in South Africa, so will this one too...maybe not now, because the balance of power is strongly in their favor, but that cannot last forever."[49]

In other words, al-Manar promotes the formation of a fifth column within Israel. As former station director Sheikh Ali Daber stated, "Our television is another type of weapon to support our resistance against the Israelis. It is a message that might just appeal to the Arabs of Israel."[50] At the same time, programs such as *The Spider's House* warn viewers that, as the demographic situation shifts in the Palestinians' favor, Israeli authorities will "remove, extract, expel, [make] people homeless, and totally destroy the Palestinian identity or the concept of Palestine."[51] Therefore, Arab Israelis are encouraged to rise up and create "armed cells" to resist Israeli occupation within the Green Line.[52] According to this worldview, "The Palestinian-Israeli citizen in the occupied lands is not at liberty to lower the flag of resistance and identity in the face of these Zionist practices. Resistance is the natural reaction."

PALESTINIAN RIGHT OF RETURN

REFERENCE VIDEO CLIPS
46 and 47

As mentioned previously, al-Manar programming explicitly asserts that the only way to bring about a just conclusion to the Arab-Israeli conflict is to grant all Palestinian refugees (whom al-Manar calls "A'idoun," or "those slated to return to Palestine") and their descendants the right of return to historic Palestine.[53] In Hizballah's eyes, Israeli aggression led directly to the displacement of refugees during the various Arab-Israeli wars of the twentieth century (see video clips 46 and 47). Hence, the group has repeatedly maintained that its war with Israel will not end until the entire Palestinian diaspora has been allowed to return. As Sheikh Hassan Izz al-Din, Hizballah director for media relations, asserted:

> All Palestinian refugees are to be allowed back to Palestine, and the Jews need to leave. Those
> Jews who were there [pre-1948] can stay. When all the Palestinians return and the Jews return
> to where they came from, we should have a referendum to see what kind of country it will be.

Al-Din maintained that Hizballah cannot accept the existence of Israel "under any circumstances" because it would be unfair to the four million refugees who reside outside of historic Palestine and their future descendants. Because "the Zionists have no right or claim to Palestine," he concluded, they "must be kicked out."

In light of these aims, al-Manar explores in detail the intricacies of international law and its application to Palestinian refugees. For example, in order to make a legal case for the right of return, programs cite international documents such as the UN's Universal Declaration of Human Rights, the Treaty for Civil and Religious Freedom, the Fourth Protocol of the European Treaty for the Protection of Human Rights and Basic Freedoms, the American Convention on Human Rights (drafted by the Organization of American States), and the Fourth Geneva Convention (1949). Most cited of all is UN General Assembly Resolution 194.[54] In highlighting this resolution, however, al-Manar ignores key portions of the relevant article—namely, the phrase "live at peace with their neighbors." Resolution 194 clearly called for Arabs and Jews to coexist peacefully. Nevertheless, al-Manar guests claim that the Arab world is "in agreement to use force in order to enforce international law," all toward ensuring the right of return for Palestinian refugees and facilitating the destruction of Israel.[55] According to this view, "No one has the right to take the Palestinian rights away—nobody."

The international community is not the only recipient of Hizballah's wrath regarding Palestinian refugees. The organization specifically blames the Arab world as well. For example, one al-Manar propaganda video includes a song titled "My Neighbors" (Jirani) that expresses Palestinian frustration at the loss of their homes, their hatred of the Jewish people for having taken away their land (and, incidentally, for killing Jesus), and their anger at the Arab world for not fulfilling its promise to recover this land. The song's lyrics, many of which are accompanied by footage of Palestinian refugees fleeing their homes in historic Palestine, include the following:

> My neighbors, where is the home to shelter me?! And where are my nation's brothers? Where
> is the home? Where is the home? Where is the home to shelter me! The Arabs will remain

stuck in the mud as long as their faith is weak....And God bless the Muslims' armies, over he who stabbed Jesus.

In a similar video titled "Leave, They Said" (Irhal qalou), voices sing:

They told me to leave. They entered my home. They killed my child....They shot me in the heart and put up a tent for me....I remained on my own, and they came in while she was dreaming and said: 'Leave, leave, leave!'

Through such videos, which often distort or sensationalize already controversial historical events, al-Manar helps to solidify rejectionist sentiments throughout the Arab and Muslim worlds.

JERUSALEM

Al-Manar has long used Jerusalem—specifically, the Dome of the Rock—as a central rallying cry for the destruction of Israel. In an attempt to incite Arabs to action, many of the station's videos are peppered with footage of individuals wearing headbands, armbands, and signs that read "Al-Quds Lena," or "Jerusalem belongs to us"—a clear rebuttal of the notion

REFERENCE VIDEO CLIP

48

that Israel has any rights to the city. As one video implores, "Uproot the night of Jerusalem! Wrest the dawn of al-Aqsa! And rise, sun of Palestine!" (see video clip 48). Here, the "night of Jerusalem" is depicted as an Israeli flag superimposed over a darkened image of the Temple Mount, while the "dawn" is ushered in by images of rockets being launched.

Given that Jerusalem is the third holiest site in Islam, controversy over its fate resonates with every Muslim. Consequently, al-Manar programming includes numerous references to the city's place in Islamic tradition. On one show, for example, Marwan Barghouti, leader of the Fatah Tanzim militias, emphasized that Jerusalem is important to Arabs and Muslims because it is the first direction in which the Prophet Muhammad prayed before switching to Mecca.[56]

In addition, al-Manar often couples images of the Dome of the Rock with footage of demonstrations taking place throughout the Arab world, particularly on the grounds of the Temple Mount. Videos feature footage of the Dome photographed from all directions, including the city of David in the south, the Mount of Olives in the east, the Western Wall's courtyard in the southwest, and the area of the Damascus Gate in the north. They also highlight scenes of Muslims praying at the Noble Sanctuary, Palestinians demonstrating and throwing stones from the Temple Mount at Jews praying at the Wailing Wall below, and Ariel Sharon visiting the Temple Mount in September 2000—an incident that many in the Arab world regard as the spark that set off the second intifada. In addition, al-Manar features footage of Israeli soldiers and religious Jews walking across the Temple Mount in order to emphasize the notion that the site is occupied.

Many of these videos also include songs that address the issue of Jerusalem. In one video titled "We Are the Victors" (Nahnu al-ghalibin), singing voices declare:

> Jerusalem is ours, the truth is ours, victory is ours. We are the victors. The land is ours, the glory is ours, Jerusalem is ours, and to her we return. Jerusalem, we sacrifice our blood for you, the land of Christ, the land of the prophets. Jews, we know the truth is on our side, from all roads we will return. From under the rocks, from between the trees, falling from the sky, we are coming back.

This particular video also features a speech by Hassan Nasrallah in which he asserts, "Your land is our land, your blood is our blood, your Jerusalem is our Jerusalem, your sons are our sons. We will return with the sunrise, and the sunrise will soon be upon us."

Lyrics to other al-Manar music videos include similar sentiments. The video "We Are a Volcano That Exploded" (Nahnu burkan tafajar) declares, "We will wear coffins until every inch of our world is liberated. She [Jerusalem] is calling us." The previously mentioned video "My Neighbors" promises, "My neighbors in Jerusalem, time brings us closer to the day of victory through God's will. And preserve for us the [first] Qibla of Islam."[57] These lyrics are accompanied by images of Hizballah parades, Palestinian and Hizballah banners, burning Israeli flags, and Israeli military actions intended to serve as evidence of brutality against Palestinians. In another video titled "Oh, Arab" (Ya 'Arabi), the narrator calls out to Jerusalem, "The Arab nation and the Islamic nation [are] with you, oh Jerusalem. God is great. God is our witness. There is no God but God." Meanwhile, pictures of the Dome are coupled with footage of Arab demonstrations, Palestinians throwing rocks, and Israeli soldiers firing into crowds of Palestinians.

One particularly powerful video on this subject—"Jerusalem, We Are Coming" (Ya al-Quds inana qadimoun)—repeatedly calls for Arabs to return to Jerusalem. As mentioned in chapter 2, al-Manar infuses such videos with footage of Hizballah guerrillas made to appear as if they are marching in the direction of Jerusalem. Images of this

REFERENCE VIDEO CLIP
49

sort suggest to viewers that Hizballah has a role to play in the liberation of both Palestine and Jerusalem (see video clip 49).

A NECESSARY ENEMY?

Hizballah fights Israel both rhetorically over al-Manar's airwaves and militarily by supporting the Palestinians, all toward the avowed goal of destroying the Jewish state. Ironically, though, Hizballah needs the conflict between Israel and the Arab world to continue indefinitely. This conflict ensures the group's relevance; the more the situation in the region deteriorates, the more support Hizballah receives. Accordingly, al-Manar programming is meant to perpetuate incitement and violence against Israel for as long as possible.

In particular, al-Manar emphasizes solidarity with the Israeli-Palestinian conflict in order to maintain Hizballah's status in the region and throughout the wider Arab world. This reliance is attributable to a number of factors. First, the chances that the Palestinian conflict will end in the near future are slim. By tying its fate to the Palestinian cause, Hizballah ensures its own continued importance in the region. Second, Shiites have historically been accorded second-class status in Arab society. By showing its support for the preeminent Arab cause, Hizballah heightens its own stature among all Arab sects despite its Lebanese Shiite background. As the lowest common denominator, the Palestinian issue is one of the few issues that the entire Arab world can rally behind (at least rhetorically). Finally, Hizballah must maintain its jihadist reputation in order to preserve an air of legitimacy among its constituents. The group was created with the explicit purpose of serving as a resistance organization, and waging war against Israel was one of its founding tenets. For Hizballah to stop its fight against Israel would mean losing its credibility and perhaps even its raison d'être.

NOTES

1. Lisa Armony, "Hezbollah's Growing Prominence in Lebanon," *Canadian Jewish News,* August 17, 2000.

2. Unless otherwise indicated, all quotes attributed to al-Manar and Hizballah personnel were obtained from the individuals in question during interviews conducted at the Beirut station on June 27–28, 2002. The titles attributed to these personnel represent the positions they held at the time of the interviews.

3. As noted in chapter 2, Muhammad al-Dura was a twelve-year-old Palestinian boy who was shot and killed during an exchange of fire between Israelis and Palestinians on September 30, 2000. Yahya

Ayash was a notorious bomb builder known as "The Engineer," responsible for training many of Hamas's future bombmakers. He was killed by Israeli forces in 1996. Izz al-Din al-Qassam was an early-twentieth-century rebel who fought against the British and their plans for a Jewish state in Palestine. Hamas's military wing, the Izz al-Din al-Qassam Brigades, was named after him.

4. Archbishop Attalah Hana, remarks made on the program *News of the Hour,* al-Manar Television, March 15, 2002.

5. Hussein al-Haj Hasan, remarks made on the program *Files,* al-Manar Television, April 2, 2002.

6. Sheikh Taha al-Sabounji, remarks made on the program *Files,* al-Manar Television, April 4, 2002.

7. Osama Hamdan (Hamas representative in Lebanon), remarks made on the program *Files,* al-Manar Television, January 16, 2002.

8. Abdullah al-Makhlafi, remarks made on the program *News of the Hour,* al-Manar Television, March 15, 2002.

9. Al-Sabounji, *Files,* April 4, 2002.

10. Badih Chayban, "Nasrallah Alleges 'Christian Zionist' Plot," *Daily Star* (Beirut), October 23, 2002.

11. Ismail Haniya, remarks made on the program *Files,* al-Manar Television, April 2, 2002.

12. Muhammad Fanish, remarks made on the program *News of the Hour,* al-Manar Television, January 18, 2002.

13. Talal Nagi (assistant secretary-general of the Popular Front for the Liberation of Palestine), remarks made on the program *What's Next?,* al-Manar Television, February 13, 2002.

14. Haniya, *Files,* April 4, 2002.

15. Muhammad Husseini (program host), remarks made on the program *Terrorists,* al-Manar Television, February 19, 2002.

16. Hashem Safi al-Din, remarks made on the program *Terrorists,* al-Manar Television, January 23, 2002.

17. Husseini, *Terrorists,* March 6, 2002.

18. Muhammad Afif, remarks made on the program *Terrorists,* al-Manar Television, January 23, 2002.

19. *Terrorists,* January 23, 2002. See also "Israeli 'Violations' over Lebanon since June 2000 Exceed 3,670," al-Manar Television, January 23, 2002, BBC Summary of World Broadcasts, January 24, 2002.

20. *Terrorists,* March 6, 2002.

21. *Terrorists,* January 16, 2002.

22. *Terrorists,* January 30, 2002.

23. *Terrorists,* February 20, 2002. The figure 103 years was likely intended as a reference to the first Zionist Congress of 1897, which met in Switzerland with the explicit goal of establishing a home for the Jewish people in Palestine. See "World Zionist Organization," in Geoffrey Wigodler, ed., *New Encyclopedia of Zionism and Israel* (Madison, N.J.: Fairleigh Dickinson University Press, 1994), pp. 1399–1404.

24. This quote matches chapter 13, verses 15–16, from the biblical book of Isaiah. Yet, al-Manar takes those verses out of context and distorts their meaning by casting them as Talmudic decrees rather than prophetic images from the Bible. The citation of "Ishaya" is probably intended as "Yishaya," the Hebrew word for Isaiah; it does not appear to indicate any actual part of the Talmud.

25. *Terrorists,* January 23, 2002.

26. Michel Semaha, remarks made on the program *News of the Hour,* al-Manar Television, April 12, 2002.

27. Hassan Nasrallah, remarks broadcast on al-Manar Television, May 23, 2002.

28. Hizballah's frustration with Arabs and Muslims for their lack of support is poignantly captured in an al-Manar video titled "Leave, They Said" (Irhal qalou), which includes the line, "I knocked on the *umma's* [community of believers] door, but they were sleeping."

29. Haniya, *Files,* April 2, 2002.

30. Muhammad Sharri (program host), remarks made on the program *Files,* al-Manar Television, April 4, 2002.

31. Al-Haj Hasan, *Files,* April 2, 2002.

32. Layla Khalid (member of the Palestinian National Council), remarks made on the program *Files,* al-Manar Television, April 13, 2002.

33. Al-Haj Hasan, *Files,* April 2, 2002.

34. Attalah Hana, *News of the Hour,* March 15, 2002.

35. Haniya, *Files,* April 2, 2002.

36. Hassan Nasrallah, speech broadcast on al-Manar Television, March 22, 2002.

37. Hassan Nasrallah, speech broadcast on al-Manar Television, March 17, 2002.

38. Khalid al-Islamabuli assassinated Egyptian president Anwar Sadat in October 1981.

39. Hassan Nasrallah, speech broadcast on al-Manar Television, March 24, 2002.

40. The title is a play on words. The Arabic word *dura* literally means "prized possession."

41. The lyrics follow along with the infamous footage of the incident, during which the boy's father attempted to shield him as they sought cover behind a barrel. Both were struck by bullets; the father survived.

42. Nawaf al-Dharu (Jordanian researcher), remarks made on "The Demographic Problem in Palestine," episode of the program *The Spider's House,* al-Manar Television, February 27, 2002.

43. Arnon Soffer, *Israel, Demography 2000–2020: Dangers and Opportunities* (Haifa, Israel: University of Haifa, 2001), p. 20.

44. Al-Dharu, *The Spider's House,* February 27, 2002.

45. On the February 27, 2002, episode of *The Spider's House,* which was dedicated to exploring "the demographic problem in Palestine," al-Manar presented statistics from the World Bank Population Index and the 1999 Israeli census in order to demonstrate how the Jewish state can be dismantled. In 2000, for example, the combined population of Gaza, the West Bank, and Israel proper consisted of 4.3 million Arabs (47 percent) and 4.9 million Jews (53 percent)—a slim Jewish majority. By 2020, this majority will disappear, with a projected 7.9 million Arabs (55 percent) and 6.4 million Jews (45 percent).

46. In 2000, Arab Israelis numbered 1.3 million and made up 20 percent of the eligible Israeli voting population. In the Galilee and the northern Negev, Arab Israelis already hold a decisive majority.

47. Al-Dharu, *The Spider's House,* February 27, 2002.

Avi Jorisch

48. Ahmed Bahaa al-Din Sh'aban, remarks made on "Zionist Identity," episode of the program *The Spider's House,* al-Manar Television, February 4, 2002.

49. Jabir Suleiman, remarks made on "Palestinian Right of Return," episode of the program *The Spider's House,* al-Manar Television, May 14, 2002.

50. Giles Trendle, "Hezbollah TV Cameras Taking Place of Rockets," *Sunday Times* (London), July 19, 1992.

51. Al-Dharu, *The Spider's House,* February 27, 2002.

52. Ibid. Al-Dharu stated that twenty-five armed cells were already active within Israel: "The future proliferation of these cells is a natural response to the Israeli policies of racism; Judaization; the use of excessive force, terrorism, and humiliation; and all other such policies."

53. A'idoun literally means "returnees." The term was officially adopted at the first Palestinian Congress in 1964 as the preferred means of referring to the refugees.

54. Resolution 194, drafted to address the "situation in Palestine," was passed on December 11, 1948. Article 11—the only portion of the document to mention Palestinian refugees—reads as follows:

    [The General Assembly] resolves that the refugees wishing to return to their homes and live at peace with their neighbors should be permitted to do so at the earliest practicable date, and that compensation should be paid for the property of those choosing not to return and for loss of or damage to property which, under principles of international law or in equity, should be made good by the Governments or authorities responsible. [The General Assembly] instructs the Conciliation Commission to facilitate the repatriation, resettlement, and economic and social rehabilitation of the refugees and the payment of compensation, and to maintain close relations with the Director of the United Nations Relief for Palestine Refugees and, through him, with the appropriate organs and agencies of the United Nations.

55. Suleiman, *The Spider's House,* May 14, 2002.

56. Marwan Barghouti, remarks made on the program *What's Next?,* al-Manar Television, February 13, 2002.

57. Qibla indicates the location toward which Muslims pray. As mentioned previously, although the current Qibla is in Mecca, Jerusalem once served this same role.

CHAPTER 5

PROMOTING MILITANT ISLAM AND THE CULTURE OF RESISTANCE

Hizballah was created in the image of the Islamic Republic of Iran, with the distinct purpose of spreading Ayatollah Ruhollah Khomeini's radical Islamic ideology. Since its inception, the group has used violence to achieve its goals and aspirations. As described in chapter 1, Hizballah freely admits its adherence to militant Islam. Accordingly, al-Manar's primary message to the Arab world is resistance (a term often used interchangeably with "jihad"). As Hizballah deputy secretary-general Sheikh Naim Qassam maintained, "Jihad is the only way to salvation, and the experience of the Islamic and the Lebanese resistance is the best proof."[1] For the Palestinians in particular, resistance is "now officially the only…option."[2] One of al-Manar's principal roles, then, is to convince viewers that resistance can actually succeed.[3]

Hizballah considers itself to be the quintessential resistance movement. Through al-Manar, the organization strives to justify, foster, and perpetuate violence against the United States, Israel, and its other enemies. Al-Manar programming helps to sustain this culture of resistance by legitimizing and inciting suicide bombing and other forms of terrorism; by justifying continued Hizballah attacks in places such as the Shebaa Farms; by glorifying Hizballah's past military successes; by lionizing Hizballah leaders; by canonizing Palestinian and other Arab "martyrs"; and by recruiting young people to its militant cause.

LEGITIMIZING SUICIDE OPERATIONS

Al-Manar programming asserts that suicide bombing is a justifiable act of resistance. As Hizballah secretary-general Sheikh Hassan Nasrallah stated in reference to the Palestinian struggle against Israel, suicide bombing is the "only weapon that we possess.…The culture of

Avi Jorisch

martyrdom is the strongest weapon....Here lies our strength."[4] According to him, Israel was forced to redeploy from southern Lebanon because

> those who love death [followers of Hizballah] defeated those who fear death [Israelis]....Those who see death and martyrdom as a way to immortal life defeated those who see death as destruction and loss....The weapon of loving martyrdom, sacrifices, and readiness for death is one that nobody can take away....Yes, we make life through death.

In light of these arguments, Nasrallah demands to know why many people insist on branding martyrdom operations as terrorism. In rebutting what he calls the "world war against martyrdom operations," he claims that suicide bombing "is a modest weapon and does not warrant that a world war be waged against it." From his perspective, a suicide bombing simply demonstrates that a "male or female youth in Palestine wants to give [a] life to his or her people. He or she wants to restore the smile of their orphan children through martyrdom." Such operations are "based on our heritage and history," both "locally and nationally."

Indeed, Hizballah and its supporters often invoke Islamic tradition as the moral justification for suicide bombing. Al-Manar has repeatedly highlighted clerics and *fatwas* (religious edicts) defending the tactic. On one program, Sheikh Babil al-Halbawi, imam of the al-Sayida Rikiyya Mosque in Damascus, asserted, "To those who say that jihad against Israel and America is suicide, I say to these people that [abandoning jihad] is actually suicide."[5] He continued, "We must overcome all barriers and obstacles in order to walk the path of martyrdom and resistance with the scholars and the martyrs and all those who are capable of fighting to achieve victory." To justify such action, he used quotes from the Quran and the Hadith (collected sayings of the Prophet Muhammad). In one such example, he analyzed a Hadith that asserts, "The ink of scholars is better than the blood of martyrs." He interpreted this line to mean the following: "The type of *ulama* [scholars]...referred to is the scholar who graduates martyrs—the scholar who walks before the masses and will end, God willing, with martyrdom, and who leads masses to the path of martyrdom."

Acknowledging the importance of religious interpretation, Nasrallah has led Hizballah in vigilantly calling on clerics to issue *fatwas* that encourage individuals to carry out suicide attacks:

> When we come to tell him [a prospective suicide bomber] that this act is religiously prohibited or that it is a sin or suicide, he will never move one step forward. No one will manage to push

him one step forward. When we talk with him in the name of God, the prophets, and the messengers, citing the holy books, jurisprudence, and religion, and tell him that what he wants to do is religiously prohibited, we block the martyrdom operations.[6]

According to him, *fatwa*s that prohibit suicide operations are issued by "religious scholars who work for the rulers. The religious scholars who issue *fatwa*s supportive of the rulers' desire, but not in accordance with the holy Quran and Prophet Muhammad's tradition, do not express religion at all." In another speech broadcast on al-Manar, Nasrallah called on Sunni and Shiite clerics to legitimize suicide bombing within the framework of Islam, claiming that "the Islamic *umma* [community of believers] is being assaulted, its dignity, its religion, its honor, its Jerusalem and its holiest sites, its incomes, its money, the future of its coming generations, they are all being assaulted."[7]

Nasrallah has also used events depicted in the Quran—including from the life of the Prophet Muhammad and his companions, some of whom died in battles for Mecca, Badr, Uhud, and Hunayn—as justification for suicide operations, reminding al-Manar viewers that these individuals gave

> life to Arabs and humanity through their blood and death....All nations throughout history made life and dignity through death. That is what Prophet Muhammad, may God's peace and blessings be upon him, taught us. This is the culture of resistance. The culture of martyrdom is the strongest weapon.[8]

Similarly, al-Manar often juxtaposes sacred text with images of "martyrdom." In one video, Quranic verses are sung in somber, quiet tones and scrolled across the screen while footage in the background shows U.S. and Israeli flags being burned, demonstra-

REFERENCE VIDEO CLIP
50

tors waving a "Down with U.S.A." sign, a suicide bomber recording his valediction, victims and rescue personnel scrambling in the aftermath of a suicide bombing, and similar images (see video clip 50).

For the most part, al-Manar takes its case for suicide operations straight to the people. Viewers are told that "the path to becoming a priest in Islam is through jihad."[9] Potential bombers are implored to focus their attention on the afterlife and on judgment day "instead of getting preoccupied with our lives here on earth."[10] Mothers are encouraged to give up their sons for God, country, and the blessings of the afterlife, to prepare them "for battle knowing that their blood will mix with the soil." In the eyes of Hizballah,

Avi Jorisch

"This belief in judgment day is the most powerful weapon in the face of technology and advanced weaponry." Such belief "drives fear into the heart of the Israeli soldier as he sits in his tank, while God guides [Hizballah's] bullets and rockets to their targets."[11]

Indeed, Hizballah insists that the afterlife is the only thing that Muslims should aspire to attain:

> There can never be absolute happiness in life....Only in the afterlife...exists true happiness....Compared to the afterlife, this life is nothing but the few drops that are left on your finger after you dip in the sea, in comparison to the sea itself. This life is simply playing around until the afterlife, where the true life begins. As the prophet once said, this life does not even equate to a mosquito's wings in God's eyes. And what are a mosquito's wings? Nothing! This life is like drinking from the sea. The more you drink, the thirstier you become. In conclusion, God warns us to be careful and not to love this life and not to get overwhelmed by it. Loving it is the basis for every misdeed.[12]

According to this view, death "takes away all suffering and pain."[13] Life, in contrast, is full of "occupation, hegemony, enslavement, oppression, and repression." "For this reason," Hizballah maintains, "when we are left to choose between these two choices, we should pick jihad and blessed martyrdom, which will lift us up to God and lift our people and our *umma* and nation after our martyrdom."

Individuals who do in fact carry out suicide bombings earn high respect from al-Manar. Besides imploring Palestinian youths to carry out such attacks, the station prominently displays pictures of past suicide bombers, provides a forum for future bombers to express their views, and airs footage of their suicide missions.[14] Young bombers' final thoughts are often videotaped just hours before the act is committed, and many of these tapes are sent to al-Manar's Beirut office and eventually aired.[15] Looking resolute and committed to the cause, male and female bombers encourage others to carry out attacks. They often hold a gun in one hand and a Quran in the other as they appear before one of several popular backdrops, which include Jerusalem's Dome of the Rock, a map of Palestine, and various organizational flags. Al-Manar frequently juxtaposes their final words with images of bombed-out buses and dead and wounded Israeli civilians and soldiers.

In particular, al-Manar emphasizes the Palestinians' ability to destroy Israel through suicide attacks. In a video titled "We Are a Volcano That Exploded" (Nahnu burkan tafajar), Nasrallah asserted:

The Palestinians can and will, through the use of their rifles, explosives, and the bodies of their martyrs, destroy this *'ar* [disgrace or shame—referring to Israel] and collapse this unjust system.

In another video titled "Rise to the Tops with Your Sword" (Halaq bi sayfak li al-qimam), he stated:

This courageous people, [who] have given over sixty martyrs and over 1,400 injured in a few days, can adopt the strategy of the knife, [whereby] a young man hides a knife, and when he approaches an occupier, he brandishes his blade and stabs and stabs with determination, and so be it if he gets killed after that.

In general, such videos place a premium on a suicide attacker's ability to kill numerous Israelis.

SELF-PROMOTION AND RECRUITMENT

In its attempts to disseminate Hizballah's resistance ideology, much of al-Manar's programming is aimed at promoting the organization itself. These efforts include both justifying and glorifying Hizballah's ongoing military activities at the Israel-Lebanon border. As discussed in chapters 1 and 2, Hizballah's guerrilla units began focusing their attacks on the Shebaa Farms area following Israel's May 2000 withdrawal from Lebanon. The group maintains that Israel's withdrawal was incomplete, and that the small agricultural zone on the border of Syria and Lebanon is occupied land that must be liberated. Since 2000, most of Hizballah's direct military attacks against Israeli forces have taken place in this disputed area.

Accordingly, al-Manar programming has long featured members of the Lebanese parliament asserting the necessity of fighting the Israelis at Shebaa. For example, Hussein al-Haj Hasan, one of Hizballah's representatives in the legislature, declared, "No matter what the Americans or the Israelis say, we will continue to fight until we recover the Farms. We have the right to continue our resistance until we get it back."[16] Muhammad Fanish, another member of parliament, stated, "The UN has no say in deciding whose land it is. Given that the Syrians and Lebanese agreed upon this division, the UN must not intervene."[17]

Al-Manar propaganda videos offer similar views. For example, a video titled "It Is My Right to Recover Shebaa" (Min haqi an astraja'a Shiba'a) includes the following lyrics:

It is my right to defend my land and kick out the occupiers; it is my right to declare my freedom and raise a flag for the oppressed; it is my right to recover Shebaa and all the captured fighters....We would not leave you with the rapist, even if many years pass.

Accompanying footage shows guerrilla operations against Israeli military bases, pictures of the three Israeli soldiers kidnapped by Hizballah in October 2000, guerrillas planting Hizballah's flag into a hill, and people celebrating the liberation of southern Lebanon.

Other self-promotional videos include similar jubilation scenes showing Lebanese citizens riding atop tanks, dancing, and participating in parades. They also show al-Khiyam prison (where Lebanese were tortured by Israeli forces and their proxy, the Southern Lebanese Army) and Bab Fatma (a point along the Israel-Lebanon border where Lebanese gather to throw stones at Israelis).[18]

Al-Manar also highlights more militant demonstrations by Hizballah and its supporters. As mentioned in chapter 4, the station shows Hizballah guerrillas marching in formation, many of them wearing arm and headbands that display slogans such as "Jerusalem Belongs to Us" (Al-Quds lena). They often wear masks over their faces as well, so that only their eyes are visible.[19]

Some of these demonstrations include young children parroting adult guerrillas, as seen in al-Manar videos such as "The Present Is Dead If You Are Not Enraged" (Mat al-Hathir ina lan taghadad) and "The Abode of Freedom" (Dar al-huria). Such children are dressed in guerrilla uniforms; some of them carry guns, and others are shown receiving kisses from Nasrallah. Al-Manar even airs footage of children undergoing military training and being inculcated with a love of suicide bombing.

Indeed, the station openly urges parents to ensure that their children are taught the philosophy of resistance. Al-Manar depicts resistance—including suicide bombing— as a family affair rather than as isolated instances of individual militancy (see video clip 51). The relatives of potential martyrs are urged to support those engaging in resistance and to embrace the prospect of sacrificing their loved ones for the sake of a greater goal. Such programming is meant to convince ordinary members of Arab society to subscribe to the culture of resistance.

Hizballah has even devised a way to provide youths with a kind of virtual military training, further encouraging them to identify with its guerrillas and with violent resistance in general. One al-Manar adver- tisement promotes the group's most recent desktop computer video

REFERENCE VIDEO CLIPS
51 and 52

game, *Special Forces,* which urges children to join the resistance and fight for the destruction of Israel (see video clip 52). According to Hizballah's website, "Stages of the game represent heroic operations executed by heroes of the Islamic Resistance against true positions fortified to protect the enemy."[20] The game is no mere historical exercise, however; it promises to provide "all that an anxious persons [*sic*] dreams of in order to participate in facing the Zionist enemy." Indeed, Hizballah's website tells players that they will become "a partner of the resistance." Similarly, the al-Manar advertisement ends with the slogan, "This is how the confrontation should be." Both the website and the al-Manar ad show scenes from the game in which the player's character—in first-person perspective—kills Israeli soldiers and destroys Israeli military facilities and vehicles. In one particularly inflammatory scene, the player is shown pointing an AK-47 at a downed figure. The figure lies below a wall hanging that shows the Star of David with bloody snake fangs emerging from its center.

Al-Manar programming also pays frequent homage to Hizballah guerrillas and leaders. Much of this attention is focused on Hassan Nasrallah, one of the party's quintessential role models. As demonstrated in previous chapters, the station gives Nasrallah's speeches ample exposure, whether through live coverage or as excerpted on various programs and videos. Nasrallah is seen in a wide array of favorable poses, including waving Hizballah flags, visiting hospital patients, meeting supporters at rallies, and delivering impassioned speeches. The most noteworthy pose shows Nasrallah holding a Kalashnikov rifle above his head, which al-Manar juxtaposes with the slogan "Jerusalem is ours." Al-Manar even highlights Nasrallah's very name—which literally means "God's victory"—in order to lend him added stature. In one frequent play on words, he is referred to as "Sayf Nasr Allah," or "the sword of God's victory."

The station also venerates Hizballah's fighters by airing footage of them waving their rifles in triumph, marching in funeral processions, capturing fortified hilltops, storming enemy lines, hurling grenades, firing weapons, and conducting rocket attacks against Israeli convoys on patrol in the hills of southern Lebanon. Most videos that employ such footage also include martial music and speeches by various Hizballah leaders. Moreover, images of destroyed Israeli tanks and Israeli soldiers on stretchers are often contrasted with images of Hizballah guerrillas made to appear larger than life. In general, al-Manar attempts to depict the guerrillas as Lebanon's benevolent protectors (see video clip 53), showing viewers that Israel would not dare invade the country again for fear of Hizballah's presence in the south.

REFERENCE VIDEO CLIP
53

Al-Manar programs also emphasize that Hizballah takes care of those who fight on its behalf, providing them with whatever assistance (financial or otherwise) they require when they have completed their service. By highlighting such benefits, al-Manar hopes to facilitate Hizballah's recruiting activities.

Avi Jorisch

Two al-Manar programs in particular are specifically devoted to this purpose. The series *In Spite of the Wounds* (Raghim al-jirah) is dedicated to former guerrillas who became members of Hizballah's Foundation of the Wounded in Lebanon after being injured in the fight against Israel. The show outlines their biographies, describes the manner in which they were injured, explains how Hizballah provided them with post-injury care, and provides insight into how they remain dedicated to a life of resistance. Each show ends with the slogan "and they still venture into jihad!" Various al-Manar officials—including Sheikh Nasir al-Akhdar, the program's director—have stated that shows such as *In Spite of the Wounds* are intended to promote domestic recruitment and foster a culture of resistance.[21]

The focus of *In Spite of the Wounds* is the reinvigorated religious and community life of wounded guerrillas. In an episode aired on March 4, 2002, Khalil and Samir Mahna, two brothers who were wounded in action, described how they received money from Hizballah to found a construction company. The destruction of Israel was an ever-present concern even in this seemingly innocuous context: the company bore the motto "together we resist, together we build." When asked about his principal motivation for remaining in Lebanon "now that Israel has withdrawn," one of the brothers replied,

> If we all leave, who will be left here to fight the Zionist enemy? Israel is not gone yet—it still exists. Israel lives on our land, in our homes. The battle is not over yet.

In Spite of the Wounds inadvertently debunks the notion that Hizballah consists of separate sociopolitical and military wings. Each episode features former guerrillas who have been integrated into society and given jobs and money to create businesses, hospitals, or other ventures. Many of these former guerrillas also play a role in educating the young. The show's January 29, 2002, episode featured Hisham Qasem, a guerrilla who was given money to start a clinic but who also works as a part-time physical education teacher. In that capacity, he encourages young children to "take an active role in the resistance movement." On February 5, 2002, the program featured Yusef Shukr, a former fighter who was given money to start an ambulance company. Clad in military fatigues during his interview, the father of eight described how he teaches his children the importance of resistance and encourages them to join Hizballah. At one point, one of his sons, no more than three years old, appears on camera holding a Hizballah flag and declaring, "Now that we freed the south from Israel, *in sha' Allah* to Jerusalem."

The effects of this sort of programming should not be underestimated. The show's March 12, 2002, episode profiled a young man named Hussein Ismail, who stated,

One of the things that excited me about Hizballah was the military activities. And through al-Manar I got to see how these resistance operations were waged. And it got me thinking, why can't I be one of these guys [who] fights?

Ismail eventually fulfilled his wish and became a Hizballah guerrilla. After being wounded in action, he visited schools to "encourage students to join the resistance movement." For those who could not join, Ismail implored them to "at least support what we do. Thank God, we are doing a good job."

A related program, *My Blood and the Rifle* (Dami wa al-bunduqiya), is dedicated to Hizballah fighters who die in the struggle with Israel. The show closely resembles *In Spite of the Wounds;* it provides biographies of guerrillas, describes the manner in which they were recruited, discusses their service in the resistance movement, and details the manner in which they died. Each episode begins with images of katyusha rockets being fired into Israel, Hizballah fighters saluting rockets, assorted other guerrilla operations, and the sound of gunfire. Simultaneously, a poem appears onscreen:

> Their blood mixed together....And their fists came joined....With both their blood and their fists they went forth to liberate the land....So the land was liberated and victory shined through....The martyrs passed away....But we continue to hear their voices....Every one of them says: 'My blood and the rifle.'

Most of the deceased guerrillas are depicted as young, healthy, religious males with similar goals: protecting their community, land, and faith. Each episode features pictures of the fighters enjoying the company of their families and friends, reading the Quran, and praying, as well as funeral scenes in which the individuals or their coffins are wrapped in a Hizballah flag. In addition to highlighting the deceased fighters themselves, the show features parents, siblings, friends, and fellow guerrillas explaining the virtues of martyrdom and the significance of sacrifice—all with the goal of recruiting new militants for Hizballah.[22]

My Blood and the Rifle provides ample evidence that Hizballah recruits youths as well as adults. For example, Majid Jafal, a fourteen-year-old boy from al-Bajuriya, joined Hizballah because "he heard the whisper of resistance calling to him"; he was dead by age nineteen. According to al-Manar, his role models were Abbas Musawi (Hizballah's second secretary-general), Hassan Nasrallah, and Ruhollah Khomeini.[23]

Avi Jorisch

The program also demonstrates that many men join Hizballah after acquiring a university education, thus disproving the idea held by many Westerners that only the poor and uneducated are lured to terrorist organizations. For example, the February 1, 2002, episode profiled a young man identified as "Mattar," who became a resistance fighter after receiving a bachelor's degree in information technology from the Arab University of Beirut. Viewers are informed that he was "drawn to Hizballah slowly until he became so engrossed in the resistance movement that it changed the course of his life." His family members and friends declare, "Our youths do not dream of luxury and comfort; they dream of life after death." Even a university official is shown saying, "We are proud of people like Mattar. I hope he sets an example for others to follow."

Similarly, the March 1, 2002, episode profiled a fallen guerrilla identified as "Khadra," whose relatives declare, "[He] was very intelligent, well liked, but life on earth was not enough for him. He was looking for something deeper, so he turned to God, to jihad in the name of God." Viewers are also told that Khadra was one of the pioneers in the resistance movement and that the "mosque was Khadra's real home, a haven." At one point in the program, a friend says, "He is a true hero."

Overall, al-Manar programming clearly conveys the message that every resistance fighter ends up a winner, whether he lives or dies. If a guerrilla lives, Hizballah ensures that he is praised and admired. If he is wounded, he is eligible for extensive benefits from the organization. If he dies, his family members will receive similar benefits and be accorded special treatment in their communities. Indeed, al-Manar's commitment to recruiting fighters for Hizballah and promoting resistance at all levels of society is clear; as the station repeatedly tells viewers, "If you die, they will remember you."[24]

NOTES

1. Nicholas Blanford, "Hezbullah Sharpens Its Weapons in Propaganda War," *Christian Science Monitor,* December 28, 2001.

2. Ibrahim al-Amin (journalist from *al-Safir* newspaper), remarks made on the program *Files,* al-Manar Television, April 2, 2002.

3. Remarks attributed to Nayef Krayem in Robert Fisk, "Television News Is Secret Weapon of the Intifada," *The Independent* (London), December 2, 2000.

4. Hassan Nasrallah, remarks broadcast on al-Manar Television, May 23, 2002.

5. Sheikh Babil al-Halbawi, remarks made on the program *Files,* al-Manar Television, April 4, 2002.

6. Nasrallah remarks, May 23, 2002.

7. Hassan Nasrallah, speech broadcast on al-Manar Television, March 23, 2002.

8. Nasrallah remarks, May 23, 2002.

9. Nasrallah speech, March 23, 2002.

10. Hassan Nasrallah, speech broadcast on al-Manar Television, March 15, 2002.

11. Hassan Nasrallah, speech broadcast on al-Manar Television, March 16, 2002.

12. Nasrallah speech, March 23, 2002.

13. Hassan Nasrallah, speech broadcast on al-Manar Television, March 24, 2002.

14. Al-Manar inserts small circular photographs of past suicide bombers in the corner of the screen during videos with titles such as "The Flag of Victory" (Rayat al-nasr), "We Are a Volcano That Exploded" (Nahnu burkan tafajar), and "Storm the Winds of Change and Crush the Elite Army" (Asif rih al-noub, ishaq jaysh al-nukhab).

15. See Greg Myre, "Palestinian Security Forces Arrest Islamic Jihad Militants a Day after Attack," Associated Press, December 29, 2001.

16. Hussein al-Haj Hasan, remarks made on the program *Files,* al-Manar Television, April 13, 2002.

17. Muhammad Fanish, remarks made on the program *News of the Hour,* al-Manar Television, January 18, 2002.

18. The content of many of these videos is clearly indicated by their titles, which include "Flag of Victory, March to Glory" (Rayat al-nasr azhaf li al-majd), "The Victory" (Al-nasr), and "Lebanon's Great Glory" (Lubnan al-majd al-athim).

19. It should be mentioned that Hizballah members at such demonstrations often give a salute that is highly reminiscent of the "Sieg Heil" salute used in Nazi Germany. On al-Manar and elsewhere, guerrillas have been shown saluting in this fashion as they participate in rallies, address the Hizballah flag, demonstrate respect for fallen comrades, and even as they fire katyusha rockets into Israel. Whether this resemblance is intentional or not, its likely psychological effect on Jewish viewers of al-Manar is not difficult to imagine.

20. See www.specialforce.net/english/indexeng.htm

21. "Hezbollah Inaugurates Satellite Channel via ArabSat," *al-Ra'y* (Amman), May 31, 2000, BBC Summary of World Broadcasts, May 31, 2000.

22. It should be noted that, in the episodes monitored for this study, the fellow guerrillas never show their faces on camera, only their backs.

23. Jafal was profiled on the program's February 15 and March 1, 2002, episodes.

24. This and similar slogans are often displayed during the commercial breaks of programs like *My Blood and the Rifle.*

Avi Jorisch

CONCLUSION

IMPLICATIONS AND POLICY RECOMMENDATIONS

Al-Manar Television is a complex phenomenon that reflects the lamentable reality currently facing Lebanon and the entire Middle East. If the existing international approach to al-Manar persists, the station's vitriolic message of hate will undoubtedly continue and even expand. Indeed, according to Nayef Krayem, al-Manar's general manager and chairman of the board, the station has ambitious plans.[1] It hopes to launch both a twenty-four-hour news channel and a number of new al-Manar channels that broadcast similar programming in English, French, Hebrew, and Russian. Although no measure—short of direct military confrontation—can silence al-Manar completely, the U.S. government can take several steps to limit the scope and effectiveness of the station's propaganda efforts and plans for expansion. Washington must implement strong measures against both Hizballah and al-Manar if it is to win the battle for the hearts and minds of Middle Easterners.

The U.S. government has been fighting Hizballah politically since the early 1980s. After years of contention, the State Department branded Hizballah a Foreign Terrorist Organization (FTO) in October 1997, while the Treasury Department labeled it a Specially Designated Global Terrorist (SDGT) entity after the al-Qaeda attacks of September 11, 2001. Those designations give Washington four key powers: first, to force U.S. financial institutions to block movement of terrorist funds; second, to impose sanctions on foreign banks that provide services to terrorist organizations; third, to block the assets of any individual or organization that associates with terrorists; and fourth, to deny visas to representatives or members of designated terrorist organizations attempting to enter the United States.[2]

Applying the FTO and SDGT labels to Hizballah is insufficient, however. Many politicians in the Arab world and Europe tend to cloud the issue of how to deal with Hizballah by treating the organization as two separate "wings": one military, the other sociopolitical. Such a distinction is both inappropriate and inaccurate; under no circumstances should it be replicated by U.S. policymakers, particularly those responsible for enforcing FTO and SDGT designations. Hizballah members themselves clearly state that the organization is one united entity with one set of goals,[3] and al-Manar's programming unmistakably confirms that the sociopolitical/military distinction is untenable. Moreover, members of al-Manar's own staff have direct and indirect ties to Hizballah terrorism and other violent activities, and the station actively solicits funds for Hizballah's guerrilla units.

RECOMMENDATIONS FOR U.S. POLICY

In light of all of these facts, the U.S. government must openly declare that Hizballah's mass media outlets—al-Manar Television, al-Nur radio, *al-Intiqad* newspaper, and various websites—are integral parts of the organization, and that they provide a powerful forum for terrorists and rejectionists while promoting the same violent goals as the so-called military wing. Washington should encourage its European allies to do the same.[4]

In accordance with this broader designation, the United States should consider taking several key steps to curb the threat posed by Hizballah and al-Manar.

• *The Treasury Department should add al-Manar to its terrorism sanctions list.* Placing al-Manar on this list would provide a catalyst for federal authorities to begin clamping down on the station's banking and fundraising activities. Such measures would be tantamount to taking action against Hizballah finances, since the organization openly acknowledges that it controls al-Manar.

• *The United States should ask the four Lebanese banks that currently hold Hizballah bank accounts—and any other banks with which Hizballah does business—to freeze the accounts in question. If these banks refuse to comply, the Treasury Department's Office of Foreign Assets Control should designate them as institutions harboring accounts of a terrorist organization. This designation would allow Washington to freeze their U.S.-based assets and block their access to U.S. markets.* On September 23, 2001, President George W. Bush issued Executive Order (EO) 13224, drafted for the purpose of "blocking property and prohibiting transactions with persons who commit, threaten to commit, or support terrorism." In announcing the order, the president declared, "We will starve terrorists of funding, turn them against each other, rout them out of their safe hiding places, and bring them to justice."[5] In accordance with this order, the four Lebanese banks that are known to hold Hizballah bank accounts—Beirut Riyadh Bank, Banque Libanaise pour le Commerce SAL, Byblos Bank SAL, and Fransa Bank—should be added to the Treasury Department's SDGT list if they refuse to freeze these accounts.[6]

As described in chapter 2, each of the four banks has received donations solicited expressly for Hizballah. Al-Manar programs have asked viewers to deposit money into accounts for funds such as the Association for Support of Islamic Resistance in Lebanon, the Intifada in Occupied Palestine fund, the Palestine Uprising fund, the Resistance Information Donation fund, and two other funds placed under Nayef Krayem's name and designated for "the resistance media" al-Manar Television. EO 13224 endows the Treasury Department with the power to disable the structure of this sort of terrorist financing, given its wide-ranging provisions for freezing assets, blocking transactions, and denying access to U.S. markets for banks that are openly linked to terrorism or that refuse to cooperate with U.S. authorities.

• *The United States should take action against any American financial institutions that continue to serve as agents for noncompliant Lebanese banks.* Major U.S. financial institutions may inadvertently be supporting Hizballah's terrorist activity by serving as "correspondent banks" for Lebanese banks that hold Hizballah accounts, including the four mentioned above. When a bank does not have a branch in a foreign country, it often allows a local bank to supervise its financial affairs there. Indeed, the four Lebanese banks mentioned above have such correspondent banks in the United States. These U.S. banks, which essentially act as agents for the Lebanese banks, include Wachovia (for Banque Libanaise, Beirut Riyadh, and Byblos);[7] Bank of New York and JP Morgan Chase (for Byblos, Fransa, and Beirut Riyadh); Citibank (for Byblos); American Express Bank (for Byblos and Beirut Riyadh); and Standard Chartered Bank (for Byblos).

Although these U.S. banks are almost certainly unwitting accomplices to Hizballah and al-Manar's activities, they would nevertheless be in violation of presidential orders and federal law if they continued to maintain ties with the organization's Beirut bankers. As mentioned previously, the SDGT designation allows the U.S. government to block any U.S.-based financial transactions made on Hizballah's part and to impose sanctions on those entities "that support or otherwise associate" with the group. Along with EO 13224, the president has several legal instruments with which to counter financing of terrorist organizations such as Hizballah, including the International Emergency Economic Powers Act,[8] the

National Emergencies Act,[9] the UN Participation Act of 1945,[10] the United States Code,[11] and UN Security Council Resolutions 1214,[12] 1267,[13] 1333,[14] and 1363.[15]

- *The Foreign Terrorist Asset Tracking Center, the intergovernmental task force responsible for uncovering terrorist financing, should begin monitoring al-Manar broadcasts for advertised bank accounts.* The task force should examine all Hizballah-funded and Hizballah-supporting media outlets for possible financial connections. Curbing terrorist financing is one of the keys to fighting a successful war on terror, particularly with regard to an organization of Hizballah's scope.

- *The United States should enforce existing laws or pass new legislation prohibiting U.S. companies from advertising on terrorist mass media outlets such as al-Manar.* In light of al-Manar's relationship with Hizballah, U.S. companies should be formally barred from advertising on the station. Any form of financial or material support for terrorist groups such as Hizballah violates U.S. counterterrorism laws. In fact, Executive Order 12947, issued on January 23, 1995, specifically prohibits Americans from engaging in transactions with Hizballah, naming it as one of several terrorist groups that "threaten to disrupt the Middle East peace process."[16]

Given that the State Department has already acknowledged al-Manar's links with Hizballah,[17] advertising on the station should be considered illegal even if the Treasury Department does not designate the station itself as an entity subject to foreign asset controls. The statutes and executive orders described above provide ample basis for investigating the legality of U.S. companies advertising on al-Manar. If such an investigation found that loopholes in U.S. law permit companies to advertise on al-Manar (or on Hizballah's other mass media outlets), then new legislation should be passed immediately to prohibit such activity.

- *Washington should begin a dialogue with European Union officials regarding European companies that advertise on al-Manar.* As discussed in chapter 2, European companies and products of note that have been advertised on al-Manar include Milka chocolate (German), Nestle's Nido milk (Swiss), Maggie Cubes (German), Smeds cheese and butter (Finnish), Picon cheese (French), Red Bull energy drink (Austrian), Gauloises cigarettes (French), and Henkel's Der General detergent (German). Moreover, al-Manar has set up its own advertising company, Media-Publi Management, to manage its advertising activities. This company has reportedly worked with more than thirty-five advertising firms, including Saatchi and Saatchi. Where possible, these firms should be encouraged to sever ties with al-Manar.

- *The United States should enforce existing laws or pass new legislation prohibiting U.S. media from purchasing footage from, or providing footage to, al-Manar. Washington should encourage Europe to do the same.* Various Western media sources, including CNN, EuroNews, BBC, and C-SPAN, have bought footage from al-Manar in the past.[18] Purchasing such footage lends al-Manar a veneer of acceptability and should therefore be prohibited. In addition, these and other media sources, along with U.S. agencies such as APTN (the Associated Press's Washington bureau) and European agencies such as Reuters, should be encouraged to refrain from selling or providing raw footage to al-Manar for use in the station's news programming.

- *The United States should enforce existing laws banning U.S. citizens and companies from working with SDGT and FTO entities.* Al-Manar employs a handful of U.S. citizens, including a Washington correspondent. According to U.S. Code, it is illegal to knowingly provide material support or resources to an FTO.[19] Hence, the U.S. government should close down al-Manar's Washington bureau (housed within the Associated Press's Washington bureau) and consider pressing criminal charges against the bureau's chief, Muhammad Dalbah. Such action would demonstrate to other U.S. citizens that supporting terrorist organizations is unacceptable and could have dire legal consequences.

  Moreover, al-Manar's main website (www.manartv.com) is hosted by a U.S.-based server maintained by DataPipe (www.datapipe.com).[20] Providing al-Manar with such services does not support freedom of the press; rather, it aids a terrorist propaganda arm in return for cash provided by terrorists. The Department of Justice should approach DataPipe for information regarding al-Manar and Hizballah's activities.

- *The United States should investigate foreign firms that have provided assistance to Hizballah or al-Manar.* Foreign firms that have worked with al-Manar in the past (e.g., Sony) should provide information to the appropriate law enforcement agencies regarding the station's operations. If these firms fail to cooperate, the U.S. government should consider imposing stiff penalties. Washington should also investigate foreign organizations that have provided media training to al-Manar personnel (e.g., Reuters; the Thomson Foundation).

- *The United States should encourage satellite package providers to remove al-Manar from their networks.* As of August 2004, al-Manar subscribed to seven satellite packages: IntelSat,[21] EutelSat,[22] New Skies Satellites (NSS) 803,[23] NileSat 101,[24] HispaSat,[25] AsiaSat 35,[26] and

ArabSat 3a.[27] As a result, al-Manar can be viewed virtually anywhere in the world.[28] Given the broad international spectrum represented by these satellite providers, the United States will have to cooperate with many of its European and Middle Eastern allies if it hopes to shut down al-Manar's satellite programming.

The channel was removed from the Australian satellite package TARBS in November 2003. Similarly, the French government is preparing to order the satellite provider EutelSat to cease broadcasting al-Manar programming in France based on charges of anti-Semitism.[29] The United States should consider exerting pressure on the other foreign satellite companies listed above to remove al-Manar from their packages. It should also follow Australia and France's lead and force IntelSat, a U.S.-based company, to remove al-Manar. Eliminating al-Manar from satellite packages could significantly reduce its viewership in North America and elsewhere.

In addition, the United States should put pressure on al-Manar's two primary distributors, the Saudi-controlled ArabSat and the French-owned Globecast (see chapter 2, "Success in Reaching Primary Audience"). If these two companies ceased to rebroadcast al-Manar, the station would not be viewable in most parts of the world. As described in chapter 2, satellite providers such as ArabSat have insisted that al-Manar programming be devoid of most, if not all, Shiite programming. Such a condition clearly demonstrates that satellite providers can impose content-related constraints on the channels that they broadcast. Hence, by not imposing additional content restraints on al-Manar programming, ArabSat and other satellite providers send an unmistakable message that the violence al-Manar espouses is acceptable. Saudi and French cooperation in this regard should be used as a litmus test for their cooperation in the war on terrorism.

Finally, some al-Manar programming is currently being broadcast in the United States through WorldLink TV, a San Francisco–based nonprofit network that repackages news from the Arab world in a program called *Mosaic*. (WorldLink is itself operated by Link Media, a nonprofit formed through a partnership of four independent media organizations.) *Mosaic* often features segments of al-Manar's English-language news broadcasts. This program is available to all U.S. households that have satellite dishes—that is, approximately 20 million homes. An estimated 2.9 million of these households have tuned in to WorldLink TV; the network does not know how many dish owners watch *Mosaic,* however. Some episodes of *Mosaic* can also be viewed via video-streaming on the internet (see www.worldlinktv.com).[30]

- *The United States should consider providing the Lebanese government with the intelligence and support it needs to enforce its own ban on foreign financing of Lebanese media and to uphold international standards of journalistic conduct.* Although al-Manar vociferously denies receiving funds from Iran or any other foreign government, it is widely known that the station does in fact receive such financing—a practice prohibited by Lebanese law. Washington should look into ways of helping Beirut apply such laws to al-Manar. In addition, the United States could help educate Lebanese television regulators about making license renewal decisions dependent on a given station's adherence to internationally accepted journalistic standards and codes of professional conduct.

- *The United States should ask Iraqi authorities to remove al-Manar's correspondents from Iraq.* Currently, al-Manar has at least two correspondents in Iraq: Ahmed al-Askari and Diyan al-Nasiri. Because their presence jeopardizes security and reconstruction efforts, Washington should seek their removal as soon as possible.

The activities of these correspondents, along with al-Manar programming in general, pose inherent dangers for U.S.-backed efforts to rebuild Iraq. The station has been calling for suicide attacks against U.S. forces since the beginning of Operation Iraqi Freedom. As more satellite dishes pour into the country during the ongoing reconstruction period, al-Manar will likely expand its anti-American message in order to arouse more negative emotions among the Iraqi people.

Moreover, Iran has launched two additional television stations aimed at Iraqi viewers (one satellite and one terrestrial). The U.S. government should warn both al-Manar and the new Iranian stations that propaganda promoting violence or hindering a successful rebuilding policy in Iraq will elicit a very sharp response.

- *In light of Syria's ongoing occupation of Lebanon, the United States should demand that Damascus end al-Manar's calls for suicide attacks on U.S. forces in Iraq and elsewhere. Syria's response should be treated as a central test for whether Damascus is cooperating in the war on terrorism.* Although the United States has long regarded Syria as a sponsor of terrorism, Damascus has reportedly cooperated with the Bush administration in fighting al-Qaeda and providing intelligence that has "saved the lives of American soldiers."[31] Yet, with Syria's blessing, al-Manar's acrimonious message is now being spread inside Iraq, inciting violence against Americans there. Although Western commentators and U.S. government officials frequently fulminate about the Qatari satellite station al-Jazeera and its pernicious effect on Arab public opinion, al-Manar represents an even more disturbing phenomenon: television programming funded and created by a terrorist organization. Syria has the power to force al-Manar to end its incitement against U.S. forces in Iraq. Theoretically, Damascus could even shut the station down if it so desired. Realistically, however, U.S. policymakers must understand that al-Manar's overall message of hate will not dissipate entirely until Syria withdraws from Lebanon and Iran ceases its support of Hizballah's radical activities.

• *The United States should pressure Egypt, Iran, Jordan, and the United Arab Emirates to close down al-Manar bureaus. It should also pressure Belgium, France, Egypt, Iran, Jordan, Kosovo, Kuwait, Morocco, the Palestinian Authority, Russia, Sweden, Syria, Turkey, and the United Arab Emirates to bar al-Manar correspondents from reporting on their soil.* The United States should make clear to allies and adversaries alike that al-Manar's message is unacceptable.

U.S. policymakers must consider the importance of crafting a sound policy toward al-Manar and Hizballah. The consequences of not doing so would be severe. Hizballah's efforts to incite Palestinian violence against Israelis have been accompanied by the provision of arms, training, and logistical assistance to suicide bombers and other terrorists in the West Bank and Gaza. Those efforts have undoubtedly had a decisive impact on the scale of violence witnessed during the intifada. Limiting al-Manar's message could lead to a more peaceful, stable environment in both the Palestinian territories and Israel.

The task of limiting al-Manar's message has taken on added urgency because of the scope of Hizballah's continuing calls for violence against U.S. forces in Iraq. The station's programming puts American lives at risk, both in Iraq and elsewhere, and hinders the prospects for peace and stability throughout the region. Washington must therefore expand its efforts to alter or silence al-Manar's message. Only then will the United States be able to make serious headway in the battle of ideas in the Middle East.

NOTES

1. Unless otherwise indicated, all quotes attributed to al-Manar and Hizballah personnel were obtained from the individuals in question during interviews conducted at the Beirut station on June 27–28, 2002. The titles attributed to these personnel represent the positions they held at the time of the interviews.

2. For more information on the U.S. government's terrorism lists, see Mathew Levitt, *Targeting Terror: U.S. Policy toward Middle Eastern State Sponsors and Terrorist Organizations, Post–September 11* (Washington, D.C.: Washington Institute for Near East Policy, 2002).

3. For example, Sheikh Hassan Izz al-Din, a member of Hizballah's Political Council and the party's director for media relations, expressed such sentiments in an interview by the author, Beirut, June 28, 2002. Similarly, in January 2002, Muhammad Fannish, a member of Hizballah's Political Bureau, reportedly stated on al-Manar, "Efforts are made to tempt the Hezbollah in order to hold it back. The objective is not to impair its political role; rather its military wing only. But I can say that no differentiation is to be made between the military wing and the political wing of Hezbollah." Quote attributed to Fannish in "Characteristics of Hezbollah's Political and Military Wings," chapter 2 in *Hezbollah: Profile of the Lebanese Shiite Terrorist Organization of Global Reach Sponsored by Iran and Supported by Syria,* Special Information Paper, Intelligence and Terrorism Information Center at the Center for Special Studies, June 2003. Available online (www.intelligence.org.il/eng/bu/hizbullah/hezbollah.htm#table).

4. France and Belgium have refused to label Hizballah—even its military wing—as a terrorist organization. Britain continues to label the military wing as an "External Security Organization," thus enabling British officials to meet with Hizballah members who sit in the Lebanese parliament and who are ostensibly part of the organization's sociopolitical wing. Although the European Union's main terrorism list designates Imad Mughniyeh, head of Hizballah's external operations, as a terrorist, it does not categorize Hizballah as a terrorist organization.

5. The White House, Office of the Press Secretary, "Executive Order on Terrorist Financing," September 24, 2001. Available online (www.whitehouse.gov/news/releases/2001/09/print/20010924-2.html). The full text of the executive order itself is available online as well (www.fas.org/irp/offdocs/eo/eo-13224.htm).

6. As mentioned in chapter 2, funds solicited for Hizballah on al-Manar can be deposited directly into these four banks using the following accounts:

   - Beirut Riyadh Bank, Ghobeiri branch (account 46-01-465000-50156) and Mazraa branch (account 79131-3)

   - Banque Libanaise pour le Commerce SAL, Ghobeiri branch, accounts 180146111266018000 and 401830

   - Byblos Bank SAL, Haret Hreik branch, account 78-2-252-133521-1-5

   - Fransa Bank, Cheiah branch, accounts 25010/69283021 and 78.02.251.133553.0.8

7. Wachovia's "International Correspondent Bank Accounts Directory" is available online (www.wachovia.com/corp_inst/page/0,,14_982_4696_2296,00.html). In addition, the Byblos Bank Group website lists all of the institution's correspondent banks by country, including five U.S. institutions (see www.byblosbank.com.lb/aboutbbkgroup/group_corspdt/index.shtml).

8. U.S. Code 50, Sec. 1701 et seq.

9. U.S. Code 50, Sec. 1601 et seq.

10. Sec. 5, as amended (U.S. Code 22, Sec. 287c).

11. Title 3, sec. 301.

12. Issued December 8, 1998.

13. Issued October 15, 1999.

14. Issued December 19, 2000.

15. Issued July 30, 2001.

16. The full text of the order is available online (http://frwebgate.access.gpo.gov/cgi-bin/getdoc.cgi?dbname=1995_register&docid=fr25ja95-126.pdf). Other relevant legislation includes the Antiterrorism and Effective Death Penalty Act of 1996 (P.L. 104-132).

17. For example, during a State Department daily press briefing on November 19, 2003, Deputy Spokesman Adam Ereli identified al-Manar as "the domestic and satellite TV station of the Hezbollah party." A full transcript of the briefing is available online (www.state.gov/r/pa/prs/dpb/2003/26422.htm).

18. Magda Abu Fadil, "Al-Manar TV: No Love for U.S. but No Help from Taliban," Poynter Online, October 23, 2001; available online (www.poynter.org/content/content_view.asp?id=16466). C-SPAN's use of al-Manar footage was witnessed firsthand by the author on March 21, 2003.

19. Title 18, Part I, Chap. 113B, Sec. 2339B.

20. Avi Jorisch, "Hosting Hate: American Internet Companies and Their Terrorist Clients," Policy Briefing, Foundation for the Defense of Democracies, September 21, 2004; available online (www.defenddemocracy.org/publications/publications_show.htm?doc_id=240569). This article includes a full list of Hizballah websites hosted by U.S. companies. In 2003, a company named Interland (www.interland.net) hosted al-Manar's website.

21. Prior to 2004, al-Manar promotional materials indicated that the station's programming was available via the satellite provider Telstar 5. Intelsat acquired Telstar 5 in 2003. See David Darling, "Telstar," entry in *The Encyclopedia of Astrobiology, Astronomy, and Spaceflight*. Available online (www.daviddarling.info/encyclopedia/T/Telstar.html).

22. EutelSat is a French-owned company.

23. According to the company website, New Skies Satellites is based in the Netherlands; it also has an office in Washington, D.C. (see www.newskies.com/emptemp/new%20skies%20final/new%20skies/product1.asp?nContentID=303).

24. NileSat is controlled by Egyptian firms. According to the company website, nine of its eleven board members are Egyptian, with five representing the Egyptian Radio and Television Union, two representing the Egyptian Company for Investment Projects, one representing the National Bank of Egypt, and one representing the Cairo Bank (see www.nilesat.com.eg/default1.htm).

25. HispaSat is owned by the Spanish companies ReteVision, Telefonica and BBVA. EutelSat is also a major shareholder. See "Marketing Terror: How Hizballah Spreads Propaganda and Hate around the World through al-Manar" (in Hebrew), Intelligence and Terrorism Information Center at the Center for Special Studies, September 19, 2004 (available online at www.intelligence.org.il/sp/9_04/almanar.htm); see also Joan Garcia-Haro, "A New Step for the Liberalization of the Telecommunications Market in Spain," *Global Communications Newsletter*, February 1998 (available online at www.comsoc.org/pubs/gcn/gcn0298.html).

26. AsiaSat's two major shareholders are CITIC Group, a Chinese-based company, and SES Global, based in Luxembourg

27. ArabSat is a Saudi-controlled company.

28. I am thankful to Reuven Erlich, head of the Intelligence and Terrorism Information Center at the Center for Special Studies, for bringing many of the details behind al-Manar's satellite packages to my attention.

29. "French Regulator Calls for Ban on Hezbollah TV Broadcasts," Agence France Presse, July 26, 2004.

30. Jonathan Curiel, "Mosaic: A Bridge to the Middle East," *Columbia Journalism Review* (September–October 2003), p. 9.

31. Adrian Pratt, "President Assad: Syria Has Aided U.S. in Terror Effort," Knight-Ridder, June 17, 2002.

APPENDIX

PROGRAMMING OVERVIEW

Al-Manar exhibits a great deal of media savvy in its daily programming, skillfully combining news, talk shows, series, family shows, and propaganda. The various categories of programming that the station offers are outlined below.

NEWS

Al-Manar's news programs have a professional appearance and include reports from correspondents in various world capitals. The station also makes extensive use of reportage and footage from the Israeli and international press. Indeed, al-Manar subscribes to several wire services, including Reuters, Associated Press Television News, Agence France Presse, and Deutsche Presse Agentur.

The station airs eight daily Arabic news bulletins (at 7:30 a.m., 9:30 a.m., 11:30 a.m., 1:30 p.m., 3:30 p.m., 5:30 p.m., 8:30 p.m., and 11:30 p.m.—all Beirut Standard Time). It also airs one bulletin in English (2:30 p.m.) and one in French (12:15 a.m.).[1] Currently, these and other news programs focus on the war in Iraq, the U.S.-led war on terrorism, Israeli activities in the Palestinian territories, internal Lebanese politics, world events, and sports.

Notable al-Manar news programs include the following:

- *Foreign Press* (Al-sahafat al-ajnabiya) provides an overview of world events as they are portrayed by the international press.
- *Reversal of Picture* (Inqilab al-soura) is a unique show dedicated to covering the Israeli press. The program highlights the Israeli viewpoint on key events, focusing on Israeli television coverage and, occasionally, newspaper reportage. The host then summarily debunks that viewpoint. The program reflects one of al-Manar's

key functions, as expressed by Sheikh Hassan Izz al-Din, a member of Hizballah's Political Council and the party's director for media relations. According to him, in order to defeat the "Zionist entity,"

> it is essential to understand that enemy first. Consequently, we must realize and understand the nature of this enemy....The more we know about them, the more we know their weak points. This makes it easier for us to confront them.

TALK SHOWS

The title of the talk show *The Spider's House* (Beit al-ankabut) alludes to an analogy often employed by Hassan Nasrallah, secretary-general of Hizballah, to describe Israel. According to him, Israel is a spider's web, and although a spider's web appears strong, it is easily destroyed with perseverance and time. Accordingly, *The Spider's House*

is dedicated to uncovering the "weaknesses of the Zionist entity" and shaping Arab public opinion, all toward the goal of facilitating the eventual downfall of Israel (see video clip 54). For example, some episodes have described how Israel will be destroyed by an increase in the Arab population and by imple-

mentation of the Palestinian right of return to all of pre-1948 Palestine. The show also claims to explore the current "identity crisis" in Israel (e.g., arguing that Russian immigrants to Israel are not really Jewish; highlighting Israel's ever-present domestic political turmoil) in order to "prove" that Israel is weak. Israel is not the show's sole focus, however. Since the U.S. invasion of Iraq, episodes have explored how to use violent resistance—including suicide bombing—to end the U.S. occupation. Other al-Manar talk shows include the following:

- *Talk of the Hour* (Hadith al-sa'a), *What's Next?* (Matha ba'ad), and *Files* (Milafat) are political talk shows that review current events, both regional and international. Guests include journalists, analysts, members of the Lebanese government, researchers, well-known members of society, and spokespersons for groups that the U.S. government has labeled Foreign Terrorist Organizations and Specially Designated Global Terrorist entities (see video clip 55).
- *Religion and Life* (Al-din wa al-hayat) is a live call-in show on which Islamic scholars and religious leaders discuss religious topics of interest to both Sunnis and Shiites.

- *The 'Nun' and the Pen*[2] (Nun wa al-qalam) is a weekly program dedicated to discussing cultural events, scientific developments, and literary achievements. It features well-known writers and scholars.

DOCUMENTARIES

- *My Blood and the Rifle* (Dami wa al-bunduqiyya) promotes and glorifies Hizballah's guerrilla operations and calls on those able to join the resistance against Israel to do so.
- *Returnees* (A'idoun) focuses on the Palestinian refugee problem. In keeping with Hizballah's ideology, the show portrays the Palestinians not as refugees but rather as citizens slated to return to all of pre-1948 Palestine.
- *Terrorists* (Irhabiyyun) is a weekly program that highlights perceived "terrorist acts" that Israel has perpetrated against the Arab world. Each episode uses the dates of its broadcast week as a window into the past, focusing on the "crimes" committed by Zionists on those same dates throughout history.
- *In Spite of the Wounds* (Raghim al-jirah) is dedicated to individuals who have been injured while fighting against Israel. Their sacrifices are glorified, as is their newfound status as pillars of society.

RAMADAN PROGRAMMING

During the month of Ramadan, al-Manar features various special programs, some of them self produced. Past examples of such programs include the following:

- *Izz al-Din al-Qassam: A Story of Jihad and Resistance* (Izz al-Din al-Qassam: Qisat al-jihad wa al-muqawama) was a four-part historical drama focusing on the life of Izz al-Din al-Qassam, an early-twentieth-century rebel who opposed British plans for a Jewish state in Palestine. The self-produced miniseries, created in 2001 at a cost of nearly $100,000, had a contemporary context as well: Hamas's military wing was named after al-Qassam. Indeed, the series reportedly resonated powerfully with Palestinian viewers.[3] Although the program had an all-Lebanese cast, Syrian filmmakers provided old military equipment, vehicles, and uniforms to give it an air of authenticity.[4]
- According to its Egyptian producer, the 2002 program *A Knight without a Horse* (Faris bi la jawad) was based in part on the *Protocols of the Elders of Zion,* the infamous nineteenth-century tract that details a supposed Jewish plot to control the world. The *Protocols* have long been touted throughout the Arab

REFERENCE VIDEO CLIP
56

world as "proof" that Jews aim to take over the region from the "Nile to the Euphrates."

• *The Diaspora* (Al-shatat), a twenty-nine-part series produced in 2003, recounted the history of Zionism from 1812 to 1948 (see video clip 56). It, too, highlighted *The Protocols of the Elders of Zion*.

MUSIC VIDEOS

Anashid, or music videos, constitute approximately 25 percent of al-Manar's satellite programming. According to one official in al-Manar's Art Graphic Department, *anashid* are meant to "help people on the way to committing what you call in the West a suicide mission. [They are] meant to be the first step in the process of a freedom fighter operation." When asked about the ramifications of making videos for that purpose, the official stated, "My job is to make the *anashid,* and the ramifications of such are not my concern. That is for my superiors to deal with. I am just doing my job." This individual and other personnel in al-Manar's Art Graphic Department declare proudly that they strive to achieve the level of professionalism seen on U.S. television networks, particularly MTV.

In general, al-Manar music videos express seven dominant themes:

• Self-promotion, which usually involves depicting Hizballah as the liberator of southern Lebanon

• The importance of resistance and guerrilla operations, and the prominent role of Hizballah's leaders (especially Nasrallah and the late Sheikh Abbas Musawi, Hizballah's second secretary-general)

• The glory of martyrdom

• Anti-American fervor

• Israel and Zionism as the embodiments of terrorism

• The future of Arab youths (in particular, the notion that Israel is killing the Arab world's future by killing its children)

• The destruction of Israel (this theme is often punctuated by references to the occupation of Jerusalem).

On average, propaganda videos of this sort last approximately three minutes. According to the station official cited above, each minute of these videos requires nearly eight hours to produce. Hence, it takes three to four days to produce a complete three-minute video. According to another worker in the Art Graphic Department, the software programs used to create these videos include Adobe PhotoShop, Premiere, After-Effect, Studiomax, Combustion, and Corel Draw.

FAMILY PROGRAMMING

- Al-Manar's sports programs include *Goal* and *Ninety Minutes* (Tis'in daqiqa) (the latter offers ESPN-style sports coverage).
- Family programs include *The New Explorers* (Al-mustakshifoun al-judud), *Muslims in China* (Al-Muslimoun fi al-Sin), and *Hands of Benevolence* (Ayday al-khayr).
- Science programs include *Horizons of Knowledge* (Afaq al-m'arifa) and *Call from the Wilderness* (Nida min al-bariya).
- Game shows include *The Viewer Is the Witness* (Al-mushahid shahid), a contest in which participants attempt to guess the names of prominent Israeli political and military figures, and *The Mission* (Al-muhima), in which contestants answer questions that gain them virtual steps toward Jerusalem. In the latter show, the first person who "enters" the holy city wins up to 5 million Lebanese pounds (U.S. $3,300), 25 percent of which goes to "support the Palestinian people."
- Children's programs include *The Little Manar* (Al-manar al-saghir), a show in the style of *Mr. Rogers' Neighborhood* that targets three- to seven-year-olds.[5]

FILLER MATERIAL

Al-Manar broadcasts a significant amount of short filler material in between full-length programs or during commercial breaks. For example, the station displays addresses and bank account numbers where viewers can send money to support Hizballah. It also lists locations worldwide where demonstrations are soon to take place.[6] In addition, slogans such as the following are displayed in Arabic and, occasionally, English and Hebrew, often accompanied by incendiary images:

- "Patience, Palestine! Only a little while is left (before you are liberated)" (Falastin sabran! Lam yabqa ila al-qalil).
- "In your death, you are victorious. The Imam Ali, peace be upon him" (Wa al-haya fi mawtikum qahirayn. Al-imam Ali 'alayhi al-salam). This saying is attributed to Ali, Islam's fourth righteous caliph and the founder of Shia Islam. Al-Manar uses it to provide encouragement to potential suicide bombers.
- "Palestine will return to us. She will undoubtedly return" (Filastin lana sat'aoud, Hatman sat'aoud).

- "The road to victory is resistance" (Wa al-nasr al-qadim muqawama).
- "If God supports you, there will be no one able to defeat you" (In yansarukum Allah f'ala ghalib lakum).

REFERENCE VIDEO CLIP
57

- "The triumph of blood is through the sword" (Intisar al-dam 'abr al-sayf).
- "Palestine is ours" (Filastin lena).
- "Jerusalem is ours" (Al-Quds lena).
- "Stronger than your tyranny" (Aqwa min jabaroutkin; see video clip 57).
- The ninety-nine names of Allah are sometimes displayed as well.

Other filler material displays the al-Manar logo accompanied by various titles:

- "The Station of Resistance" (Qanat al-muqawama).
- "The Station of Arabs and Muslims" (Qanat al-Arab wa al-Muslimin).
- "The Station of Knowledge and Dialogue" (Qanat ma'arifa wa al-hiwar).

WEBSITES

Al-Manar has two official websites containing programming details, pictures, propaganda music videos, and speeches by Hassan Nasrallah:

- www.manartv.com (this site is hosted by a U.S.-based server maintained by DataPipe)[7]
- www.dm.net.lb/almanar

NOTES

1. Al-Manar plans to add another English news bulletin at 11:00 p.m. As Ibrahim Musawi, editor-in-chief of al-Manar's English news desk, explained, "More people in the West would be able to watch" the station's English news broadcasts if they were available at a reasonable hour.

2. "Nun" is the Arabic equivalent of the letter "N."

3. Nicholas Blanford, "Hezbullah Sharpens Its Weapons in Propaganda War," *Christian Science Monitor*, December 28, 2001.

4. Bassem Mroue, "TV Station of Lebanon's Hezbollah Guerrillas Shows Historical Drama with Relevance to Today's Palestinian Uprising," Associated Press, November 28, 2001.

5. Nayef Krayem (al-Manar's general manager and chairman of the board), interview by author, al-Manar Television station, Beirut, June 27, 2002.

6. Such locations have included Belgium, France, Lebanon, and other Western and Arab countries.

7. Avi Jorisch, "Hosting Hate: American Internet Companies and Their Terrorist Clients," Policy Briefing, Foundation for the Defense of Democracies, September 21, 2004; available online (www.defenddemocracy.org/publications/publications_show.htm?doc_id=240569).